The Alien World

THE
Unexplained

The Alien World

Major UFO cases examined and assessed

Editor: Peter Brookesmith

BLACK CAT

Acknowledgements

Photographs were supplied by Agence Angeli, Agence France Presse, BBC, BBC Hulton Picture Library, Janet & Colin Bord, Peterborough Public Library, P. Daly, Mary Evans Picture Library, Flashbacks, Flying Saucer Review, Fortean Picture Library, GEOS, GSW, Timothy Good Collection, Gwynedd Archives Services, ILN, H. Jacobs, Guy Jouhaud, P.J. Klass, Kobal Collection, Kal Korff, London Express, Mansell Collection, MacDonald Futura, NASA, R.M. Owen, M. Piccin, Picturepoint, Popperfoto, Jenny Randles, Terry Rice, Sandhurst Studios, Scala, Science Photo Library, Paul Snelgrove, Frank Spooner, Syndication International, D. Tansley, John Topham Picture Library, Stanley Travers & Partners, T. Verdal, Arthur Williamson Studios, Young Artists/Tony Roberts.

Consultants to	Picture Researchers
The Unexplained	Anne Horton
Professor A. J. Ellison	Paul Snelgrove
Dr J. Allen Hynek	Frances Vargo
Brian Inglis	**Editorial Manager**
Colin Wilson	Clare Byatt
Editorial Director	**Art Editor**
Brian Innes	Stephen Westcott
Editor	**Designer**
Peter Brookesmith	Richard Burgess
Deputy Editor	**Art Buyer**
Lynn Picknett	Jean Hardy
Executive Editor	**Production Co-ordinator**
Lesley Riley	Nicky Bowden
Sub Editors	**Volume Editor**
Mitzi Bales	Lorrie Mack
Chris Cooper	**Assistants**
Jenny Dawson	Ruth Turner
Hildi Hawkins	Sarah Reason

First published 1984 by Orbis Publishing Ltd
Reprinted 1988 by Macdonald & Co (Publishers) Ltd under the Black Cat imprint

Macdonald & Co (Publishers) Ltd
3rd Floor, Greater London House
Hampstead Road, London NW1 7QX

a member of Maxwell Pergamon Publishing Corporation plc

Material in this publication previously appeared in the weekly partwork *The Unexplained*, © 1980-83

ISBN 0-7481-0143-8

Printed in Belgium

The Unexplained

The Unexplained Price UK £1.95 IR £2.50 Aus $4.75 NZ $5.50 SA R4.75 Singapore $9.00 USA and Canada $4.75.

How to obtain your copies
Copies are obtainable by placing a regular order at your newsagent or by taking out a subscription. Subscription rates: for six months (13 issues) £27.50; for one year (26 issues) £53. Send your order and remittance to Punch Subscription Services, Watling Street, Bletchley, Milton Keynes, Bucks MK2 2BW, being sure to state the number of the first issue required.

Back numbers UK and Eire: back numbers are available from your newsagent or from **The Unexplained** Back Numbers, Orbis Publishing, 20/22 Bedfordbury, London WC2N 4BT at cover price. **Australia**: back numbers are available from **The Unexplained** Back Numbers, Gordon & Gotch (Aus.) Ltd., 114 William Street, PO Box 767G Melbourne, Vic 3001. **South Africa, Europe and Malta**: back numbers are available at cover price from newsagent. South African readers should add sales tax.

Note: back numbers are obtainable subject to availability of stocks. Whilst every attempt is made to keep the price of the issues constant, the publishers reserve the right to increase the stated prices at any time when circumstances dictate.

Published by Orbis Publishing Ltd,
Orbis House, 20/22 Bedfordbury
London WC2N 4BT

Contents

Introduction

IT IS A CURIOSITY of the history of unidentified flying objects that most writers on the subject state that the phenomenon started in 1947, with Kenneth Arnold's legendary sighting of a number of airborn discs while he was flying across the state of Washington. In fact, UFOs have disturbed or astonished the world's populace for hundreds, if not thousands, of years. What really started in 1947 was the systematic *study* of the phenomenon – and for one very good reason which we will return to later.

Today, attitudes to UFOs are much more complex than the belief – or hope or fear – that little green men are skimming about our skies in solid, 'nuts-and-bolts' machines. In Britain and in the United States a loose movement of researchers has come together under headings such as 'the new ufology', and, roughly speaking, they are suggesting that the phenomenon is indeed paranormal – inexplicable by normal logic – but that it is essentially Earthbound, possibly even the product of the human mind in some way. The new ufology occupies the middle ground between the nuts-and-bolts school who believe in the extra-terrestrial hypothesis (ETH) and those who suggest that the UFO experience is only another form of delusion, a sophisticated form of hallucination.

Even that is a simplification however, for there are ufologists who fully believe in the nuts-and-bolts interpretation, yet who refuse to believe the extra-terrestrial hypothesis and speak darkly of government conspiracies and secret military hardware. At the other end of this scale are those who are perfectly prepared to agree that the UFO experience – especially the kind that includes apparent contact with aliens – is 'all in the mind': but, they say, someone or something *out there* is feeding this information to selected individuals for purposes that we can only guess at.

A variety of such interpretations of the UFO data is presented here. What perhaps needs to be said, given the differing analyses existing, is that in fact one person's UFO experience may be entirely different from another's – one person may report a sighting of a nuts-and-bolts craft that doesn't conform to 'normal' specifications on the same night and at the same hour that another has an inexplicable hallucination of being taken aboard an enormous UFO and meeting tall, benign blond strangers. Both these people have become 'UFO cases'. Both have undergone experiences that were completely real to them at the time, but each has been through something completely different from the other. The questions that remain are: Do their different experiences have anything in common? and: What do these experiences mean – if anything?

What is perhaps the next most obvious question to ask is why anyone should assume that extra-terrestrials are involved in the first place. Among ufologists there are a number of astronomers, and almost all of them are mildly embarrassed by the extra-terrestrial hypothesis. After all, they reason, the conditions under which life is likely to arise elsewhere are very narrow. They involve the formation of a star that will be curiously like our own Sun – one that will be neither too large and bright (and so burn itself out quickly) nor too small and weak (and so be too feeble to warm its planets to the proper temperature). Stars of the right size will last the appropriate length of time, but they may be part of a planetless double-sun system as opposed to a star-and-planets arrangement. Always supposing that these conditions are met, primitive life has to have time to evolve in to *intelligent* life. It then has to undergo a transformation no less radical than our own Renaissance in order to acquire the necessary desires, riches and technological means to reach out to other stars, other peoples.

The odds against this happening are, it will surely be obvious, enormous. It is even less likely that such a civilisation will have developed to this state at a time when their technology and awareness matches or surpasses our own – even supposing that they had the resources to mount such expeditions in the first place. After all, it is within the technical capability of Earth to explore space, even to communicate with possible other races by radio, but by and large we choose to spend our money on other projects. Anyone 'out there' who chances to come across the remains of our deep-space probes will not do so for hundreds or even thousands of years and, unless they have solved the problem of beating the time barrier, any reply they may send could similarly take centuries to reach us.

Put these rather bald and grim facts against the sheer variety of seemingly alien contacts that people have had on Earth, and we are clearly in difficulties at once; the idea that vast numbers of different civilisations are (more or less quietly) getting in touch with us simply doesn't stand up to common sense. A single civilisation may have done so by a massively remote chance; perhaps they have been keeping an eye on us for thousands of years before trying to announce their presence. But 'contactees' tell such different stories, describe such different entities and offer so many conflicting opinions that one rapidly finds the whole proposition untenable, or at least highly unlikely – since the possibility remains that somewhere in this mass of data and experience there is a kernel of truth, could we but discern it.

Still, *why* should people want to believe that aliens are out there watching us? The answer may lie in the fact that the flying saucers seen by Kenneth Arnold caught public attention just as governments were seriously thinking about space exploration for the first time. But that was also a time when the cold war was at its height, only just after the most appalling destruction had been let loose in the shape of the atomic bomb, and when a large number of people suddenly felt deeply insecure about their own futures and the future of humanity. It was comforting to many to believe that another race, either by example or by positive guidance, might solve the perennial and very frightening problems that humanity had made for itself. Perhaps it is no accident that much of what is supposed to be alien philosophy concerns itself with living in peace and brotherhood.

One more point leads us to suspect the validity of the case for the ETH, and that is the way in which so-called alien technology is never more than a step in front of our own. This suggests that a purely human imagination is at work, elaborating on facts that have already become common knowledge. (The counter, and perfectly logical, argument is that the space people, being excellent anthropologists, do not want to upset us by pushing us too far, and carefully refrain from introducing us to ideas or achievements that are not already familiar to us.)

However unassailable the logic is, however, the evidence for the ETH is not very convincing. One of the most grandiose claims for contact with space beings has been that put forward by the Swiss farmer Billy Meier, who supplied not only large numbers of very elegant photographs of the craft they arrived in, but thousands of pages of communications. Unfortunately the photographs included very few of the space people themselves, and those that did surface were of ladies strangely reminiscent of Herr Meier's girlfriends. Not only that, but the pictures of the 'spaceships' involved do not stand up to rigorous analysis, despite the vehement claims of the photographer's supporters. No less problematic is the famous French case from Cergy-Pontoise, which made the front page of no less a paper than the London *Times* when the story first broke. On close inspection, large holes appear in the tale that are none too credibly papered over by the embarrassed mutterings of those concerned.

Even so, there is clear evidence that people have experienced something very strange indeed – and not only in our own time. The 'scareship invasion' of monstrous airships over the British isles just before the First World War is a case in point. And it is made scarcely less interesting by the fact that a similar wave of sightings was made in the United States – particularly in the wide-open spaces of the prairie states such as Nebraska and Iowa – during 1896 and 1897. The American sightings are fascinating because they illustrate the point about 'alien' technology being only a step ahead of *existing* knowledge – since the airship at that time was a very new and crude vehicle. The British, on the other hand, were well aware of German developments in airship design by 1913 and were besides engaged in a massive arms race with their continental rivals. Was some form of mass hysteria or mass illusion at work in both the United States

and Britain at the time? And if so, what would have caused such a psychological phenomenon in America? Or was some more bizarre form of paranormal manifestation going on – some type of mass precognition?

We are now edging into the territory of the 'new ufology'. A classic case that has caught the attention of this movement is the lights produced by Mrs Mary Jones during her part in a religious revival in rural Wales in 1905. To say 'produced' of course presumes that somehow she was in control of them, whereas there are no real grounds for supposing that they did not appear because of forces – divine or otherwise – that as much as anything were also in control of her.

The new ufology has even gone as far as to suggest that some cases of UFO sighting are a peculiar combination of psychic and material forms. This theory says that the belief in UFOs can become so strong – whatever the original stimulus may be (and it may be something as banal as an aircraft mistaken for a UFO, or as actual as a dream about UFOs) – that the thought takes on a material reality. This virtually solid 'thing' may then be witnessed by people who are quite independent of the original source. This is a mind-boggling idea, but given what we know about poltergeists and other spontaneous psychic phenomena, it may not be as far-fetched as it seems at first. Quite how it can be researched and verified however, is an altogether different matter.

Perhaps the creepiest of UFO-related experiences is the encounter with the Men in Black (or MIB) who appear to UFO witnesses after the event. Once more the interpretation will depend on the predilections of the analyst or ufologist involved, but the characteristics of these shadowy figures are unnerving, to say the least. It is precisely because they are so weird that they raise all the questions we have been asking about the true nature of the UFO phenomenon. Men in Black call on UFO witnesses and tell them to remain silent (often the witnesses don't otherwise we'd never know about MIBs). They behave like stereotype G-men out of bad B-movies, and dress in outdated clothes into the bargain. They make threats they cannot, or do not, fulfil. Yet they know things that only the witness could know. On the other hand, they don't quite look human and in some cases seem to have no idea of what is acceptable behaviour in polite society. Are they then, even if only occasionally, actual government representatives (behaving with deliberate strangeness for some reason of their own)? Are they part of some enormous hoax – or even practical joke? Are they an hallucinatory reaction to an unreal but deeply disturbing event? Or are they none, or part of these things.

It is this very range of possibilities that makes ufology so fascinating: in it, all shades of the paranormal are present.
PETER BROOKESMITH

The story of the 'Welsh triangle'

The astonishing series of events in Dyfed in 1977 drew UFO enthusiasts and investigators from all over the country. But, says HILARY EVANS, the west Wales flap was not quite what it seemed

UFOS IN THE SKY and on the ground. Cars pursued by orange footballs. Glowing cigars hovering over schools. Discs flying into solid rock and vanishing between sliding doors. Silver-suited entities with no faces stalking across fields and peering through cottage windows. Mysteriously malfunctioning cars, television and radio sets. Visits from sinister aliens with psychic powers. The teleportations of entire herds of cattle. Such, if the reports are to be believed, are just some of the extraordinary events that occurred not in some far-off land but in peaceful, homely Wales, and not at some distant time but as recently as the spring of 1977.

Are these astonishing reports to be believed?

In so accessible a region, and at so recent a date, there should be no problem about ascertaining the facts. Yet already discrepancies are apparent that may never now be resolved. The local paper, the *Western Telegraph*, did an excellent job of reporting the events as they occurred, but the affair attracted wider attention. It brought into west Wales reporters from the national press and television; it lured investigators, some competent and some not; it enticed unscrupulous authors. Between them they created a confusion that is well-nigh impossible to disentangle. Accounts vary from one version to another; dates are incorrectly stated; the order of events is confused. And, as we shall see, the personal bias of some investigators, the desire of certain reporters for a 'good story' regardless of truth, the gullibility of some witnesses and the suggestibility of others – all these have combined to add distortion to confusion. Does this mean that the west Wales 'flap' doesn't deserve our attention? On the contrary, it remains a classic case – but not quite in the way it has been made out to be.

The build-up to the events of 1977 had begun before the close of the previous year. Already residents of this remote corner of Wales were reporting UFO sightings on a scale that led Randall Jones Pugh, a local British UFO Research Association investigator who was interviewed by a journalist on 13 January, to forecast: 'The country is in for a spate of such incidents.'

His prediction was confirmed on the afternoon of 4 February, when he received a telephone call from the mother of a pupil at

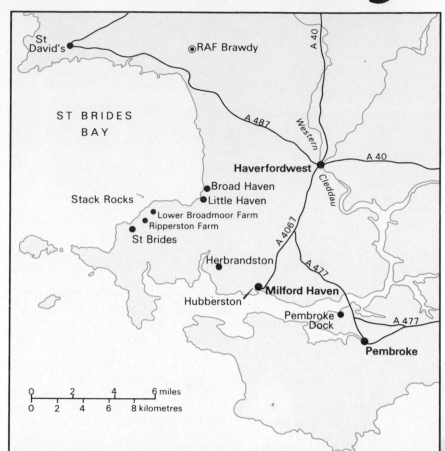

nearby Broad Haven primary school, saying that her son, along with a dozen other children, had seen a UFO that afternoon, over a period of some hours, on the ground close to the school.

Although, the Broad Haven school incidents were not the most sensational events of the west Wales flap, they were the first to alert the general public to the fact that something extraordinary was taking place in the locality. And, unlike some of the later occurrences, the facts – if not the explanations for them – are reasonably well-established.

The first sighting took place during the lunch break, when a group of boys aged between 9 and 11, who were playing football in a field beside the school, noticed an unfamiliar object in another field close by. It was apparently at ground level and was partly obscured by trees and bushes, so that they could discern only its upper portions; they could see enough, however, to feel sure that it was a UFO. Some of the boys rushed into the school with the news; others came out to see what it was. Eventually there were 15 children who saw the object.

They described it as being 'as long as a coach or maybe a bit longer'. One description

Left: the area of Dyfed in west Wales where a wave of UFO activity was reported over a period of several months in 1977

Below: the primary school at the village of Broad Haven in Dyfed where 15 children claimed to have seen a UFO on 4 February 1977. The object was first seen at lunchtime in a nearby field; when the children came out of school at 3.30 p.m. it seemed to have disappeared, but then it rose into the air from behind a bush. However, when the field was examined later no traces of a landing could be found

Above: some of the drawings made by Broad Haven schoolchildren to illustrate what they had seen. Many of the witnesses described a silver, cigar-shaped object with a dome on top; some reported a flashing light on the dome, and that the object seemed to be humming. Six of the children said they saw one or two beings near the UFO and described a small, silver-suited man with long, pointed ears

was of two saucers stacked one against the other to make a sort of dome, with a round 'ashtray' added to make a smaller dome on top. One boy saw three or four windows around the edge, on top of the dome; others thought they saw 10 or 11. Several thought they saw a light flashing on top, and one witness claimed that it was red. One saw a door in the side, with a runway leading down from it. Some, but not all, heard a humming sound. In addition, six of the witnesses reckoned that they saw one or two entities near the object. 'We saw something come out of it. It had a helmet,' said one. A second described 'a silver man with spiked ears', while a third added, 'He wasn't a very tall person, and he didn't look very nice either.'

The children watched the object for some 20 minutes. Two of them went to tell the headmaster, but he does not seem to have been sufficiently convinced to come to see for himself, though one boy 'was nearly crying because he was scared that he was going to be disintegrated or something'.

At 2 p.m. they went back into class, to re-emerge at 3.30. Naturally, they returned to the field at once to see if their UFO was still there. At first they couldn't see it and tried to get closer, though this meant crossing a fence and a stream. But just then the UFO popped up again from behind a bush, and they all took to their heels. This time they reported, 'The cigar object seemed to be tugging an object which was silver.' Again it disappeared behind a bush.

Many of the children told their parents about the incident when they got home. Randall Jones Pugh's name was familiar in the region as that of the local UFO specialist, so it was natural that he should be the first to be contacted. At 6 p.m. he visited the site with one of the boys. By now, however, it was raining heavily, and the light was fading fast,

Below: witnesses point out the site of the alleged UFO landing (right) for newspaper reporters. About two weeks after the first sighting, a teacher watched a large silvery object glide away from the same spot, and a couple of hours later two canteen workers at the school saw a strange object in the field. The canteen ladies, however, firmly believed that what they had seen was a tanker from the nearby sewage works; they visited the site with their husbands the next day to look for tyre marks, but found none

so he returned next morning, with a reporter from the *Western Telegraph*. However, no traces of the landing were to be seen.

News of the occurrence spread rapidly, and the tiny seaside village immediately found itself the centre of intense interest. On Monday the headmaster overcame his initial scepticism and asked the witnesses to draw what they had seen. By this time the children had had plenty of opportunity to discuss the matter both among themselves and with enquirers and reporters: the consensus was that they had seen a silver, cigar-shaped object with a dome and possibly a light.

It was in much the same terms that, two weeks later, one of the teachers described a

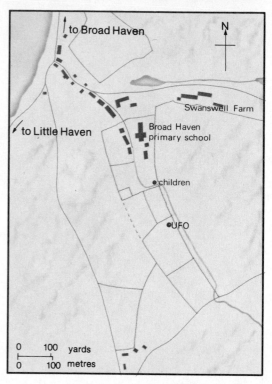

large object that she had seen on the same spot, though she glimpsed it only for four or five seconds and in pouring rain. She was about to call others when it glided away with a humming sound. Later that day two other adults, canteen workers at the school, noticed an object in the same place, saw a figure climb into it and watched it move up a slope. They did not think for one moment that they were watching a UFO but considered that it was a vehicle associated with the sewage works close by. Even when it was pointed out that it would have been very difficult for any type of vehicle to get to that location, they refused to accept that they had seen a UFO.

Despite their scepticism, the Broad Haven school sighting, taken at face value, appears to be quite convincing. There are, however, some additional factors that investigators at the time failed to take into account: these we shall consider when we have looked at some of the other sightings reported from the area. For from then until the late summer hardly a week was to go by

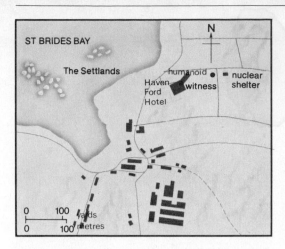

St Brides Bay / The Settlands / humanoid · / Haven Ford Hotel · witness · nuclear shelter / N / 0 100 yards / 0 100 metres

Left: the site of a UFO landing reported by Mrs Rose Granville, proprietor of the Haven Fort Hotel (below), on 19 April 1977. The witness claimed to have seen two humanoids apparently examining something close to their craft. Local BUFORA investigator Randall Jones Pugh has pointed out that there is a nuclear shelter at the site for the use of the Royal Observer Corps. Did this attract the ufonauts?

came from outside and was reflected off the walls. He got up, looked out of the window and saw that the sky was orange.

Immediately outside here I saw two silvery-coloured objects. The first was like a very large Easter egg, about 4 feet [1.2 metres] in diameter, and it was swinging back and forth a little above and behind the chimneys of the house opposite. I then saw an object like a man in a silvery boiler suit about 40 feet [12 metres] above my window. It was at least 7 feet [2 metres] tall, and it hung stationary, on a level with the 'Easter egg'. Its attitude was in the position of a free-fall parachute jumper. . . . It hung

without some fresh incident being reported in the neighbourhood. Public interest was kept simmering not only by newspaper reports but also by widespread discussion, by visiting reporters for press and television and by investigators from UFO organisations. For the next six months or more, UFOs were to be front-page news in the area.

Here, taken from among 45 cases described in minute detail in reports and interviews, not to mention others reported in less detail, are a handful of selected incidents.

On 10 February two 12-year-old boys saw a UFO in a field near Haverfordwest grammar school. It was a blue flashing light, seen at a distance of about 130 yards (40 metres). One boy threw a stone at it, whereupon it took off; as it did so, an orange cigar shape about 16 feet (5 metres) long materialised beneath it. It hovered for a while, then vanished.

On 16 February Graham Howells, a 13-year-old schoolboy of Pembroke Dock, saw a bright, metallic object hovering over Pembroke school as he arrived in the morning. Although the weather was misty, he claimed a clear view of the object, which had a dome in the middle which was dark grey most of the time, but flashed to a dazzling white about every five seconds. It resembled a plate with a burnt fried egg on it. Around the rim of the 'plate' it had greeny-yellowish lights and what seemed to me to be retro-rockets. The 'plate' seemed to be revolving as well. . . . I'm sure it wasn't a helicopter or a weather balloon.

On 13 March Stephen Taylor, aged 17, saw a UFO at about 9 p.m. It was a glowing light with an orange halo around it. He went to the house of some friends to tell them about it, but they did not believe him. About half an hour later, in a field, he saw a dome-shaped UFO about 20 feet (6 metres) high and stopped to look at it. Then a figure like a tall man approached, wearing a semi-transparent suit and a kind of spaceman's helmet. 'I was so frightened,' Stephen said, 'that I just took a swing at it and ran.'

On 7 April, Cyril John, aged 64, woke at about 4.45 a.m., disturbed by a strange orange light pulsating in his bedroom. It

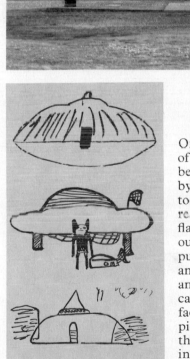

Four remarkably similar versions of the Broad Haven UFO, drawn by children from the school. The witnesses made the drawings independently, but not until three days after the sighting, so they would have had plenty of time to discuss what they had seen

motionless in the sky, face downwards, for about 25 minutes. The 'egg' then moved up above roof-level and glided away sideways, as did the figure.

On 19 April Mrs Rose Granville, proprietor of the Haven Fort Hotel, was just going to bed, at about 2 a.m., when she was disturbed by a strange humming sound. At first she took it for the central heating, but then she realised that it was something unfamiliar. A flash outside her window caused her to look out: she saw a bluish light circling around, pulsating as it went. She got her binoculars and saw an oval object resting on the ground and, near it, two figures in 'whitish, plasticated' clothing like boiler suits; they had no faces. When the local newspaper printed a picture of a hoax spaceman and suggested that this was what she had seen, she wrote an indignant denial.

With cases such as these being reported almost every week, it is not surprising that as early as 17 February investigator Randall Jones Pugh commented to a local reporter: 'There's certainly a minor flap down here.' On 28 April he told the same paper that he was planning a book on the sightings. No doubt he was encouraged in this venture by a further series of events, which were even more extraordinary: the astonishing incidents reported by the inhabitants of Ripperston Farm, just south of Broad Haven.

A giant, faceless humanoid, the strange teleportation of cattle, and a car-chasing UFO – just some of the many phenomena allegedly experienced by the Coombs family at Ripperston Farm. But how much of what was reported actually took place?

DURING THE AUTUMN OF 1977 an enterprising hotelier in west Wales was offering special weekend breaks for UFO investigators. Enthusiasts would be free to use the hotel facilities all night long, and an expert would guide them to the most favourable locations for UFO spotting, though sighting was not guaranteed. 'Pembrokeshire is quite a way ahead in this sort of thing,' the hotelier observed, and she professed herself 'flabbergasted at the number of people who have written or telephoned'.

What was drawing the attention of UFO enthusiasts, not only from Britain but also from abroad, was the continuous flow of remarkable reports from what the newspapers were naming 'the Broad Haven triangle'. Serious ufologists have learned to be cautious about 'flaps'. Periods when more

The Ripperston Farm riddle

than the usual number of reports come in may genuinely represent an increased level of activity, but it may simply be that the publication of reports encourages witnesses to come forward who would otherwise have kept their experiences quiet. No more incidents occur; it is just that more are disclosed. And there is the further possibility that news about sightings may stimulate some people to have imaginary experiences.

Such possibilities are anathema to those ufologists who are convinced that all UFO sightings are grounded in physical fact and deny that there may be a psychological aspect to such experiences. But that some kind of 'contagion of ideas' was operating in west Wales during the spring and summer of 1977 is suggested by many of the reports – most of all by the series of astonishing events that were alleged to have taken place at Ripperston Farm, focusing on the Coombs family. So completely did these events capture the public imagination that three books were wholly or in large part devoted to them, as well as extensive coverage by press and television. Unfortunately, this resulted in so much contradiction and confusion that the true facts are often impossible to establish. In what follows the most probable version of the truth has been selected, but frequently it has been a matter of choosing between contradictory accounts, and absolute accuracy cannot be guaranteed.

Billie Coombs was a herdsman, one of three men responsible for looking after the dairy herd at Ripperston Farm on behalf of the farm manager, Richard Hewison, who lived at neighbouring Lower Broadmoor

Farm and was in turn responsible to the company that owned both farms. Mr Coombs and his wife Pauline lived with their five children in a cottage on Ripperston Farm. Immediately next door was another cottage, where Brian Klass, also a Ripperston employee, lived with his wife Caroline.

Although Pauline Coombs reported some earlier UFO experiences, the first major event occurred on 16 April. She was driving home one evening after dark, with three of her children, when her 10-year-old son Keiron, who was in the back seat, reported a strange light in the sky. It was about the shape and size of a rugby ball, luminous, yellowish, with a hazy, greyish light underneath and a torch-like beam shining down from it. Keiron told his mother that the light had u-turned and was following them. The object caught up with the car and travelled along beside it, at which point the car lights started to fade. Near the house the engine cut out altogether, so that Mrs Coombs had to coast the rest of the way. She ran in to call her husband. He and their eldest son, Clinton, came out just in time to see the UFO heading out to sea. When Mr Coombs tried to start the car, it functioned perfectly.

A few weeks later Mrs Coombs reported

Left: Ripperston Farm, near St Brides Bay in west Wales, home of the Coombs family who reported many seemingly paranormal events in the spring and summer of 1977. One of the striking aspects of this case is that Brian and Caroline Klass, whose cottage adjoined that of the Coombs, did not see or hear anything unusual at this time – or at least chose not to publicise their experiences

Above: the road leading to Ripperston Farm along which Pauline Coombs was driving on the evening of 16 April 1977 when, she claimed, the car was chased by a UFO (left). She and the children were terrified, and their fear increased when, as they approached the house, the car engine and lights cut out completely so that they had to coast the rest of the way home

seeing another UFO from her kitchen window. It was about 20 feet (6 metres) in diameter and rested about 3 feet (1 metre) off the ground. Silvery in colour, it had antennae and a tripod undercarriage. It took off towards the sea, leaving a circular 'burn mark'. On another occasion two of the younger children claimed to have seen three UFOs in the sky, circular in shape and with domes. One was only about 50 feet (15 metres) above the ground, and from it a ladder was lowered, down which the children saw a silver-suited figure climb. The UFO also dropped a bright red, fluorescent box-like object into the grass

of the field: later the children looked for the box but it had apparently disappeared.

On 22 April Mr and Mrs Coombs were watching a late-night film on television, despite interference, which was particularly bad that evening. At about 11.30 p.m. Mrs Coombs became aware of a glow outside the uncurtained sitting-room window. An hour or so later her husband saw a face at the window. 'It was a man – but a terrible size,' he later reported, estimating the height of the figure at nearly 7 feet (2 metres). The creature was wearing a white suit. Its face – if it had one – was concealed behind a kind of black visor.

Terrified, Mr Coombs telephoned first the farm manager, Richard Hewison, and then Randall Jones Pugh, the local British UFO Research Association investigator. Pugh advised him to inform the police. Hewison came round at once, followed by the police, but they found no trace of the intruder. About three weeks later a similar figure was sighted by the eight-year-old twins. They were out in the fields, 'playing roly-poly in the grass', when they saw an entity that they described in almost the same terms as their parents had – it was dressed in silver, with a black head. It walked past them, about 50 feet (15 metres) away, then it disappeared, apparently having walked through a barbed-wire fence.

A strange disappearance

Of all the events that were reported from Ripperston Farm, the most bizarre was the seemingly supernatural movement of cattle. On several occasions, Billie Coombs found that the cattle – sometimes only one or two animals, but frequently the entire herd – had disappeared from the yard. On at least one occasion he received an angry telephone call from a neighbouring farmer asking him to come to collect his herd. Mr Coombs insisted that the animals had been properly fastened in, adding that he had secured the bolt with binder twine as an extra precaution. To escape in the way indicated the herd would have had to move past the cottage: yet neither he nor his wife had heard a sound. On one occasion, he reported, there simply had not been enough time between the moment at which the cattle had last been seen and the moment when they were reported at another farm for them to have traversed the distance in any natural way. The implication had to be that they had somehow been spirited from one place to the other. The cattle were badly frightened, and the milk yield was down.

This extraordinary movement of cattle presents the toughest challenge to our credulity. The UFO and entity sightings, remarkable as they are, fall within a commonly accepted range of phenomena, but this movement of animals seems to belong to a different class.

It is not, however, entirely without precedent. In his book *Haunted houses* (1897),

John Ingrams describes a strange report from Birchen Bower, near Oldham in Lancashire. At this house a macabre custom was observed. A former owner, terrified of being buried alive, had refused to allow her body to be buried. Instead she left instructions that it should be embalmed and brought to the house every 21 years, where it was left in a granary for a week. This had an extraordinary effect on the livestock:

> In the morning, when the corpse was fetched, the horses and cows were always found let loose, and sometimes a cow would be found up in the hay-loft, although how it came there was, indeed, a mystery, as there was no passage large enough to admit a beast of such magnitude. . . . A few years ago, when a cow belonging to the farmer then tenanting the place was found in the hay-loft, it was the firm belief of many thereabouts that supernatural agency had been employed to place it there. . . . How the cow was got up was a mystery to everyone, whilst that blocks had to be borrowed from Bower Mill to let it down through the hay-hole outside the barn was an equally well-known fact.

The *Daily Mail* of 18 May 1906 noted, in the course of a report on a disturbed house: 'A horse vanished from the barn and was found in the hay room. A partition had to be knocked down to get him out.' And in April 1936 the Italian journal *Ali del Pensiero* reported:

> Phenomena of incendiary infestation have been recently established on a farm in Prignano (Salerno); fires broke out spontaneously, destroyed household objects, and burned persons and

Above: from her kitchen window Pauline Coombs saw a UFO flying towards the sea

Right: map showing the position of Ripperston Farm in relation to that of Lower Broadmoor Farm. On several occasions Billie Coombs reported that cattle had mysteriously disappeared from his yard – even though he had secured the gate – only to turn up at Broadmoor Farm a half-mile (800 metres) away. Local BUFORA investigator Randall Jones Pugh (below) visited the farm but could find no explanation for the mystery

animals. Bricks and stones fell in the rooms, although the windows were closed. There was spontaneous displacement of objects. A pair of oxen were even found to have been carried from one stall to another without human agency. . . . A doctor and psychical researcher found a 16-year-old girl with strong mediumistic faculties who was the involuntary means of the striking phenomena.

This last case indicates that poltergeist activity was diagnosed, which raises the question of whether a similar agency was at work at Ripperston. If so, it was a particularly powerful one: the teleportation of an entire herd of cattle transcends any poltergeist phenomenon ever reported. Nonetheless, other events reported from Ripperston might be seen as supporting the poltergeist hypothesis. It is noteworthy, for example, that the place seemed to exert a highly malevolent influence on mechanical objects. Apart from the alarming failure of Pauline Coombs's car at the climax of her frightening UFO chase, Billie Coombs reported that he

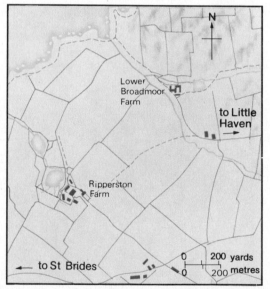

had to replace his car five times during 1977 and that they suffered an even higher accident rate with television sets. Again, the family's electricity bill was so high that they asked the Electricity Board to inspect the meters. No fault was found.

The suggestion that psychic forces may have been at work is supported by the earlier history of Pauline Coombs, who was by faith a Roman Catholic. Some time before coming to Ripperston, the Coombs family had been living in a caravan at nearby Pembroke Dock. Strange manifestations began to occur. Every evening, from the inside of the caravan, Mrs Coombs could see a life-size apparition of the Virgin, who was wearing a white dress. She had a rosary tied round her waist and was holding the child Jesus. Later the figure became that of Jesus on his own. The figure remained for half an hour. Word got around, and soon every evening there was a crowd of sightseers hoping to catch sight of the phenomenon. Eventually, the owner of the caravan had it destroyed because he was annoyed by the flow of visitors. As reported, this incident is very unsatisfactory. Caravan owners do not usually resort to destroying their own property, even for such a reason. However, for our purpose, the suggestion is clear that there was already some quality about Pauline Coombs that might make her prone to strange experiences.

The proliferation of incidents at Ripperston Farm made it a focus of interest for reporters and investigators on and off throughout the spring and summer of 1977. And perhaps it was only to be expected that sooner or later those ubiquitous figures, the sinister men in black (see page 30), should be reported as turning up at the farm. One day, so the account alleges, an unusual car drove up, but silently, so that no one heard it. It contained two men who were remarkably similar in appearance. One of them got out, immaculately dressed in a neat grey suit and gleaming shoes. He was inspecting the cattle yard when Caroline Klass first saw him from her cottage next door, yet in some uncanny way he was instantly beside her, asking where Pauline Coombs was, somehow knowing that Mrs Klass was not her. He is described as speaking with a foreign accent and as having something alien about him. He possessed 'large, penetrating blue eyes which seemed to go right through her and examine her thoughts'.

The report alleges that the Coombs's eldest son, Clinton, was in the neighbouring cottage at the time but was too frightened by the visitors to open the door to them; instead, he bolted it and hid upstairs. Failing to get an

Above: Pauline Coombs at the window through which she and her husband saw a humanoid at about 1 a.m. on 23 April 1977. Mrs Coombs had noticed a 'glow' at the window an hour or so before, but decided not to mention it to her husband because she believed he would think she was 'suffering from nerves'. But then Mr Coombs saw a creature, a silver-suited man of 'a terrible size', pressed right up against the window (right). The police were called, but they found no signs of the intruder

Below: a silver-suited entity was seen by two of the Coombs children

answer to his knock, the man returned to Mrs Klass and pressed her for further information, though he seemed to know her answers before she uttered them. Then he asked her to show them how to reach their next destination, and the two men set off in their strange vehicle. A few seconds later Mrs Coombs arrived in her car. Investigators commented on the fact that although there was no turning off the lane by which she had come, Mrs Coombs had not passed the two men. How could she have missed them?

If things had indeed taken place as this report suggests, we would have good reason to believe that something genuinely uncanny had occurred at Ripperston that day. However, more objective investigation reveals the

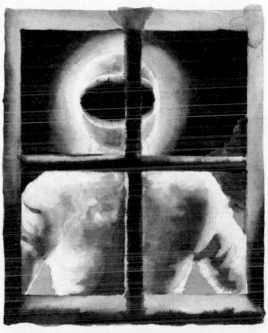

'evidence' to be a hotch-potch of misleading statements and mischievous inventions. The two men were not foreigners. They were not uncannily identical. Their questions were perfectly natural. Moreover, far from knowing that Caroline Klass was not Pauline Coombs, their first action was specifically to ask if she *was*. Clinton was not hiding in the house, terrified. And as for the question of why Mrs Coombs had not passed their car as she drove up, the explanation is perfectly simple – Mrs Klass had indicated to them a short cut that would enable them to reach their destination more quickly, and it led away from the farm by a different road.

In short, the whole episode, as it has been reported, is an irresponsible distortion designed to create a sensational story out of a simple and perfectly natural incident. And this was far from being the only incident in the west Wales sightings in which the true facts were somewhat different from those that were reported.

The west Wales sightings form one of the most complex and richly documented UFO cases on record. But the facts were often markedly different from those that were reported

THE REPORTS OF UFO activity in Dyfed in 1977 provide a dazzling variety of incidents and a small army of witnesses, as well as phenomena ranging from distant sightings to close encounters, with all manner of picturesque happenings on the side. Small wonder that the media moved into the area in force, and that innumerable newspaper and magazine articles and television programmes should by devoted to the astonishing events in this one small corner of Britain.

But in the end it was the sheer scale of this blaze of publicity that revealed the weaknesses of the accounts offered to the public. Had there been but one version, it might have been accepted as gospel, but there were several, and they all differed in detail and contradicted one another in interpretation. No reader with his wits about him can fail to notice the number of discrepancies and, once alerted, he starts to notice other defects – assumptions too easily made, questions not asked, awkward facts lightly passed over. Finally he realises that in some respects the investigation has been woefully incomplete,

One of the many reports of UFOs in Dyfed in 1977 was made by 13-year-old Deborah Swan, who claimed that while she and some friends were on a UFO hunt they were terrified by a 'brilliant gleaming silver' object, the size of a football, that was hovering in a field close by. But did the children really see a UFO? Or did they simply want to believe they had seen one because so many others seemed to have done so?

winter afternoon: 'It was a very dull day, but I did see something,' said one witness, which suggests an uncertain, indistinct sighting that would hardly permit the precise pinpointing of the landing site.

However, it does not seem justifiable to accuse the children of deliberate hoaxing. The fact that, when their teachers did not believe them, they took the brave step of handing in a petition at the police station speaks well for their sincerity. Undoubtedly, they saw something that they could not identify. What that something was we may never know for certain, but it seems probable that the suggestion of the two canteen workers who saw an object at the same spot, that it was a vehicle associated with the sewage works located close by, is the correct one.

Why, then, did the children suppose that they were seeing a UFO? Here we move from physical to sociological considerations. Two days before, several schoolboys at Penarth, Cardiff, claimed to have seen a cigar-shaped UFO. The following day – the day before the Broad Haven sighting – the *Western Telegraph* reported that another cigar-shaped UFO had been seen at nearby Hubberston primary school, for between 10 and 15 minutes, by children playing football. There is no need to suppose that the Broad Haven children were consciously seeking to emulate

The truth about the Welsh triangle

while in others the facts have been distorted or exaggerated almost beyond recognition.

In the light of more objective investigation into the west Wales sightings it is possible to see just how much truth subsists in the accounts given to the public, and to reassess some of the events outlined in preceding articles.

The Pembrokeshire UFO 'flap' may be said to have started at Broad Haven primary school, and it is appropriate that reassessment should start with a visit to the site of the alleged sighting. Straight away we are in for a surprise. The reports hardly emphasise how densely the site is covered with bushes and trees, so that any sighting must have been largely screened. It would have been impossible for the children to have seen the UFO in its entirety, so the sketches that they drew the following Monday must be regarded as largely make-believe. Again, we find that the field is in a narrow valley, overlooked by a number of houses. It has always seemed improbable that a UFO should remain in a field in broad daylight for three hours and more – there is no precedent for such a sighting. The proposition becomes even more improbable in the light of the fact that its alleged location was within constant sight of a semi-circle of houses. It should also be recalled that the events all took place on a

the others, but it is evident that the idea of UFOS was very much in the air at the time and might have come naturally to the minds of schoolchildren confronted with an unfamiliar object. The boy who was scared that he might be 'disintegrated' by UFO entities – like the other witness who thought he could distinguish 'retro-rockets' on the side of a UFO – already had in his mind the raw materials from which an imaginary UFO could be constructed.

The Broad Haven story immediately stimulated the public imagination. The next week's *Western Telegraph* noted: 'Reporters, photographers and television cameramen arrived in a two-day procession to see the starstruck youngsters, who were only too willing to repeat their fantastic story.' Even those who did not believe that story were made aware that curious things were going on; while those who *were* ready to believe drew fresh encouragement from this flare-up of interest. Soon local investigator Randall Jones Pugh was telling reporters, 'The phone hasn't stopped ringing since the Broad Haven sightings. People are beginning to come forward now that they realise nobody is going to take the mickey out of them.'

How many of the sightings reported to Pugh and others in this way have any basis in fact it is probably now impossible to ascertain. But as one leafs through the files of the local newspaper, presumably read by a high proportion of the local populace, one is struck by the way in which the subject was kept simmering throughout the spring and summer of 1977. Week after week the correspondence columns included letters presenting views for or against. The reports were both serious and objective, never sensational and at the same time never mocking. This fact in itself would have been sufficient to create a favourable soil in which the false could be nurtured along with the true.

With the national media, on the other hand, it was a different matter. Absurd tales, heavy with exaggeration, were concocted by

Stack Rocks in St Bride's Bay, which allegedly attracted the attention of 'silvery' humanoids in October 1977. The figures were seen climbing on the rocks by Mrs Rose Granville (above), who claimed to have observed them through binoculars from the Haven Fort Hotel. However, the hotel is about 3 miles (5 kilometres) from the rocks and it is unlikely that she would have been able to make out much detail at this distance

journalists who dropped in for brief visits, then returned to London to write about the terrified locals who dwelt in the 'terror triangle', as the *Sun* named it. It is in the light of this emotional climate that cases such as the following must be evaluated.

On 14 April 13-year old Deborah Swan of Herbrandston was playing with friends in the park at about 6.30 p.m. Since there had been so many reports of weird happenings, they decided to see if they could find this 'outer space thing', but having gone a little

way from the park, two of them turned back because 'it began to get scary.' The others went on, under fences, across a potato field, down a bank – and then, as Deborah later reported:

There was something in the field opposite out of the ordinary. I have never seen anything like it before in my life. . . . I thought it was my eyes playing a trick – but it wasn't. The most astonishing thing about it was the colour, which was a brilliant gleaming silver. The shape was like a round football, and also the movements. . . . It moved at all angles – backwards, frontwards, left to right . . . as we moved, it moved as well. We then ran back as fast as we could. . . . We didn't hesitate to look back, but just kept running.

What did Deborah and her companions see? Was it really a UFO or just an hallucination? Was it a misperception? Was it pure imagination or deliberate fiction? One thing is certain: it is altogether without precedent for anyone to go looking for UFOS and to run across one within a few minutes. And yet Deborah's story was accepted literally at the time by all those who were supposed to be conducting an objective investigation into the facts.

It was the happenings at Ripperston Farm that were the most widely publicised of the west Wales sightings. How do they stand up to objective investigation? Right away, one is struck by the fact that the Coombs family had neighbours who lived not simply nearby but in a cottage that was actually joined to their own. Throughout the period of the alleged incidents Brian and Caroline Klass were living right next door, working alongside Billie Coombs. Yet it is a fact, however hard to believe, that not one single reporter or investigator bothered to ask the Klasses for their view of the matter. On the occasion of the only event in which they were directly involved, the sinister visit of the two 'foreigners', false statements were put into Mrs Klass's mouth to give the incident a totally misleading slant.

Invention clearly embroidered the matter of the 'miraculously' transported cattle. Both the farm manager and Billie Coombs's fellow worker testify that the Ripperston cattle were continually getting loose and finding their way on to neighbouring farms. Could they get past the cottages without anyone hearing? Certainly, declares Billie Coombs's neighbour. When there was a wind blowing they wouldn't hear a thing, particularly if the television or radio were on.

And there are other happenings at Ripperston that, looked at objectively, turn out to be less than inexplicable. There is the mysterious force that allegedly acted on mechanical objects, destroying five cars in the course of a year. Those who knew Mr Coombs have pointed out that a cowman doesn't have the resources to buy that many new cars. What he did was to purchase more or less condemned cars from a scrap yard, get them working as best he could and drive them until they finally fell to pieces. A similar explanation accounts for the high accident rate among the family's television sets. As for the abnormally high electricity bill, a neighbour alleges that the Coombs family were forever leaving the central heating fully on while doors and windows were open.

One of the most sensational incidents was the appearance, on the night of 22 April, of a mysterious entity at the Coombs's sitting-room window. On this occasion there is no doubt that something really did happen; the farm manager whom Mr Coombs telephoned in the middle of the night was convinced that he was genuinely frightened. But by what?

Some time earlier two local men were passing the Haven Fort Hotel, in whose grounds the proprietor had recently reported seeing a UFO and a couple of entities. On an impulse, they decided to play a trick on her. They proceeded to tramp around the building in a sinister fashion, using a torch to enhance the effect. It seems probable that it was these same jokers who were later responsible for the Coombs 'entity'. Although the identity of the jokers is widely suspected, they have not openly admitted their complicity, so the explanation must remain conjecture only. However, the hoax explanation is generally accepted in the area today.

Space does not permit an item-by-item exposure of similar errors and exaggerations, but the sensational Stack Rocks sighting must be mentioned. Unfortunately, the discrepancies between the various reported accounts of this incident are even more glaring than usual, so it is impossible to say quite what happened or in what sequence. What is supposed to have occurred is roughly as follows.

A flash in the sky

Early one evening in October Pauline Coombs was driving to Ripperston with her mother and some of the children when her mother saw a disc-shaped UFO fly overhead towards Stack Rocks, which stand out at sea some distance from the mainland. The UFO circled the rocks, then dived into them through what appeared to be sliding doors.

Alarmed, they continued on their way. Hardly had they arrived home when the telephone rang. Mrs Granville, of the Haven Fort Hotel, had seen a flash in the sky, which had prompted her to fetch her binoculars to examine Stack Rocks (which, incidentally, were her property). She had seen figures climbing about on the rocks, and wondered if Mrs Coombs had seen any such thing? Mrs Coombs immediately set off from the farm towards the cliff, accompanied by some of the children, to obtain a better view.

According to the reports, they came back confirming Mrs Granville's sighting. However, closer investigation reveals that what happened was that on their return from the cliffs some of the children ran on ahead of their mother. Caroline Klass, their neighbour, asked the boy Keiron if they had seen anything, to which he replied, no, of course they hadn't. But when Mrs Coombs arrived she insisted that they had indeed seen entities clambering about the rocks on what appeared to be stairs.

What are we to make of this? Again, a visit to the site certainly helps. The Haven Fort Hotel is some 3 miles (5 kilometres) from Stack Rocks, which makes it improbable that any movement could be seen in detail, particularly as it was evening, and the side of the rocks facing the mainland was in shadow. Additionally, the side facing the hotel is at an angle of 90° from Mrs Coombs's viewpoint, so it is unlikely that she would be able to see the same thing. Mrs Granville's explanation

At the time of Mrs Granville's sighting on Stack Rocks, members of the Coombs family were driving home to Ripperston Farm when they saw a silver, disc-shaped UFO circle the rocks, then disappear into them as if through sliding doors. A telephone call from Mrs Granville prompted Pauline Coombs and some of the children to go to the cliff top to look at Stack Rocks, and they too claimed to see figures climbing there. Subsequent investigation of the rocks, however, revealed no evidence of UFO or humanoids

for her alarm at the flash and her subsequent inspection of the rocks is not convincing, for the sky above St Bride's Bay is continually flown over by jets from the RAF base at nearby Brawdy, Stack Rocks being a mark in the flight path of aircraft approaching the airfield. Flashes in the sky over Stack Rocks must occur many times every day.

One notes, too, that the Coombs's first sighting must have been made from a moving car that was travelling along a bumpy, un-surfaced road, from which the rocks can be glimpsed only intermittently. At that point they must have been about 2 miles (3 kilo-metres) away. A BBC investigator visited the rocks to see if there was anything that might have given rise to the sighting. He found nothing. It is noteworthy, though, that from the approximate angle at which the Coombs family must have seen the disc dive into the rocks, there are two large rock slabs, sep-arated by a darker area, that could con-ceivably lend themselves to interpretation as a pair of sliding doors.

Finally, what value can be placed on Pauline Coombs as a witness? It has been suggested that she might have been a natural psychic, but it is also possible that she was either very suggestible or highly imaginative. Some time after the events of 1977, and shortly after a television programme featur-ing a notable UFO contactee, Mrs Coombs confided to Caroline Klass that she, too, had been taken for a trip in an alien spaceship.

The investigation that has led to the disclosures made here was undertaken speci-fically for *The Unexplained*, not with the intention of debunking the reports but simply in order to establish the real facts. The unearthing of such a farrago of exagger-ation and omission, of gratuitous distortion and outright falsehood, was as unexpected as

Above: Josephine Hewison, who reported seeing a huge object 'like a squashed jelly mould' in a field at Lower Broadmoor Farm (top). Researchers were convinced by her straightforward and objective account of the sighting, and there seems to be little reason to doubt that she did indeed see something paranormal

it was dismaying. Inevitably, one is forced to ask whether there is any substance whatever in the west Wales flap of 1977.

Fortunately, not all the findings were as disillusioning. There seems no reason to doubt that a good many of the witnesses who submitted their experiences to the press or to the British UFO Research Association rep-resentative, Randall Jones Pugh, did so in good faith and were reporting events that may well have been genuine UFO sightings. Of all these cases, one must stand for the rest.

A little before 8 a.m. on Saturday, 26 March, Josephine Hewison of Lower Broad-moor Farm, whose husband Richard man-ages the farm that includes Ripperston, was standing at her bedroom window. In a field just beyond the drive that circles around the front of the house she saw a massive object some 50 feet (15 metres) wide, large enough to hide, almost completely, a greenhouse that stood behind it. It had a round, three-tiered shape – a broad base, then a rounded ridge with a dome above. The whole thing, in Mrs Hewison's words, was 'rather like a squashed jelly mould'. It was smooth, bulbous, aluminium-coloured. There was no sound, no indication of activity. It was full daylight but overcast, which invalidates the theory that she might have been dazzled by sunlight reflected from the greenhouse.

She gazed at it for about two minutes, then realised that she ought to tell somebody else. She went to wake up her children, but when she looked out of the window again, the object had vanished.

Curious and unforgettable

There is no way to confirm or refute Josephine Hewison's testimony. But a visit to the site makes it clear that there is nothing there that she could have misinterpreted. Either she saw something real or she was hallucinating – and there seems no reason to suppose that she was hallucinating. Today her view of the incident is a measured, objective one. She knows that she saw some-thing that morning, and she continues to think it likely that she saw something 'real'. Though some reporters described her as 'terrified', what she saw didn't frighten her at all. It was simply a curious and an unforget-table experience.

The story of the west Wales flap is a sad revelation of human nature. Some of those involved emerge as simple-minded, only too ready to believe what they are told without questioning. Others, though claiming to be objective investigators, have shown them-selves to be incompetent or prejudiced. Some who have proffered evidence are to be seen as simply unreliable, others may be considered fraudulent. Just a few people, like Josephine Hewison, seem to have had genuinely para-normal experiences. But because of the way in which the affair was treated, the truth has been buried beneath every kind of error and evasion, fiction and fraud.

Of the many Welsh religious revivals, that of 1905 was unique. For at its heart was the preacher Mrs Mary Jones who, as KEVIN McCLURE describes, could summon up miraculous lights over the Welsh countryside

PROBABLY THE MOST remarkable series of phenomena ever reported in Wales were the mysterious Egryn lights. Yet few people today (even among those interested in paranormal happenings) have heard of them or of their apparent inspiration, the visionary preacher Mrs Mary Jones. The background to the appearance of inexplicable lights seen around Mrs Jones was the Welsh Methodist revival of 1905, which was led by the young evangelist, Evan Roberts.

Wales had long been the home of such intense and emotional revivals, involving large numbers of converts who experienced drastic, if temporary, changes in their way of life as a result. By September 1904, when the latest revival began, a traditional pattern was already well-established. Since the Great Revival of 1859 – when a staggering 110,000 converts were claimed – there had been important local revivals in 1866, 1871, 1882–83, 1887, 1892 and 1893.

A study of the 1905 revival describes the 'mystic doctrine of salvation by personal experience, in which realisation of sin led to an emotional crisis which convinced them [the converts] that they had been saved.' Preachers denounced sinners from the pulpit, cajoled and promised the glories of heaven for those who repented. Packed services ran for hours at a time.

But this particular revival quickly showed unusual features. Evan Roberts based his personal 'testimony' on his alleged visions from angels and from Christ himself. Methodism is not a faith that takes kindly to mysticism or other 'Popish' traits and Roberts was severely criticised for his emphasis

Above: Mrs Mary Jones, focus of the miraculous lights

Right: a sketch of the scene at Pensarn where a train driver saw a light shoot in 10 directions while Mrs Jones preached nearby

Below: the modest little chapel at Egryn as it was during the revival of 1905. One well-attested event was the coming of a 'star' from over the sea to flood the chapel with light

Fire within and without

Right: map of the Egryn district, where Mrs Jones's phenomena occurred during the peak of her ministry in 1905

on personal revelation of this literal kind. Perhaps this censure explains partly why few chose to remember the revival in later years; after all, claims of visitations from holy persona are not uncommon in Catholic centres such as Lourdes in France or Fatima in Portugal. The good Methodists of Merionethshire had no taste for pilgrimages and shrines.

Yet the controversial activities of Evan Roberts paled into relative insignificance beside the wonders that came to be associated with Mrs Mary Jones, a 35-year-old farmer's wife from Egryn, a hamlet between Barmouth and Harlech in Merionethshire (now Gwynedd).

Seeing is believing

Experiences such as Evan Roberts's visions are often subjective, only experienced by one person. Consequently it is hard to prove whether or not they really happened. But Mary Jones did more – she inspired phenomena that others could see. She experienced visions, found herself surrounded by moving lights, received messages from 'The Saviour in bodily form'. She firmly believed herself to have been chosen to be 'the accepted medium for the spreading of the Revival throughout Merionethshire.' These experiences led her to commence a nightly mission in her local chapel and soon others also began to witness lights, to see visions – and they were converted.

The first of many independent reports comes from the *Cambrian News* of 13 January 1905. Reporting her successful conversion work, it mentions that until recently the lights she has claimed to have seen had been regarded 'as one of her own inspiring thoughts', but that they have now been seen by others.

> Last week Mrs. Jones attended a meeting at Pensarn, where hundreds of people congregated. The chapel can be seen from the railway and as a train, driven by a Machynlleth man, was passing, a strange light was seen shooting out of ten different directions, and then coming together with a loud clap. 'Never do I wish to see anything like it again', said the driver in relating his experience. Both he and his mate saw the light.

Clearly Mrs Jones and her lights were by now well-known along the Cambrian coast, and the appearance of independent testimony attracted several journalists from respectable newspapers to the little Islawrffordd farmhouse that lies between the sea and Tal-y-bont halt on the railway. Once there, they attempted to establish the background of this seemingly ordinary country woman.

They found that, like so many others who are the centre of psychic or paranormal phenomena, she had been far from happy in her childhood and adolescence. Orphaned at

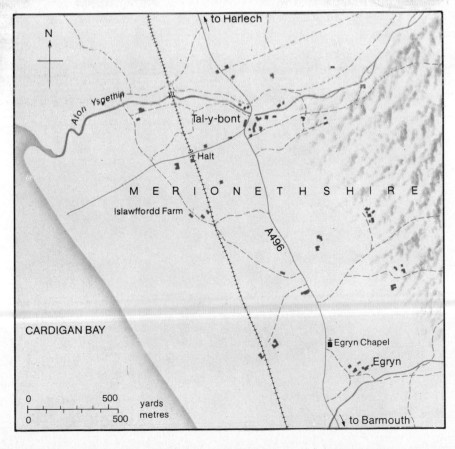

N

to Harlech

Afon Ysgethin

Tal-y-bont

Halt

M E R I O N E T H S H I R E

Islawffordd Farm

A496

CARDIGAN BAY

Egryn Chapel

Egryn

0   500
|—|—|—|—|—| yards
0   500   metres

to Barmouth

an early age, she was cared for by her sister. Then her sister died, too, and Mary lost her lifelong faith in God.

But during the first stirrings of the revival in South Wales she underwent a dramatic, though solitary, conversion experience and returned to regular attendance at the Egryn chapel. Gradually she became more involved; then her visions began, and she decided to start her own daily meetings at the tiny chapel. She told Beriah Evans, a Caernarvon journalist, of her experiences at this time, and accounts appeared in the *Manchester Guardian* and the *Barmouth Advertiser*:

> The first night's mission was marked by the appearance for the first time of Mrs. Jones' 'Star' and 'Lights'. The star was heralded by a luminous arch, of the character of the 'Aurora Borealis', one end resting on the sea, the other on the hill-top – a distance of well over a mile [1.6 kilometres] – bathing the little chapel in a flood of soft effulgence. The star soon after appeared, its light flooding the chapel itself.

In the same articles, Evans wrote of the apparent 'intelligence' of the star or lights, which seemed to respond to both individuals and situations.

The star has seemed to rest above particular houses, whose roofs are thrown out in bold relief amid the surrounding darkness. When this occurs in the Egryn district a convert or converts invariably turn up at the next meeting from that particular house. . . . It [the star] glows placidly on the roof of the chapel where her service is held, and when it does so the spiritual character of the meeting is very marked.

The Reverend Elvet Lewis, writing for the Christian *British Weekly*, records similar events of lights appearing over the houses of those who were to be converted. He stated that a Wesleyan minister in Barmouth could confirm them and, therefore, everyone else should take the reports seriously.

As the journalists arrived, many of them became witnesses to the lights, and were able to publish the names and addresses of other responsible witnesses. Perhaps because he was a local man, Beriah Evans was the first into print. On 9 February 1905 this account appeared in the *Daily News*:

> After tea, we had two miles [3 kilometres] walk to the chapel. Besides myself, there were present the Rev. Llewelyn Morgan, Harlech, the Rev. Roger Williams, Dyffryn, and one other – Mrs.

Above: artist's impression of the strange phenomena surrounding Mrs Jones's first night as an evangelist. While she was preaching inside Egryn chapel a luminous arch, something like the *aurora borealis*, began to take shape with one end resting on the sea and the other on a hilltop a mile (1.6 kilometres) away. Soon afterwards a 'star' appeared, filling the chapel with soft light

Above right: journalists witnessed an intense, sparkling 'star' flash over a nearby railway crossing, apparently caused by Mrs Jones's presence

Right: Mrs Jones's 'star' was frequently seen to hover over a specific house, and invariably this preceded the conversion of one or more of the inhabitants, usually the following day

Jones came in dressed for her journey. Going outside, she immediately returned, remarking: 'We cannot start yet, the Light has not come.'

Five minutes later she went out, returning promptly to say: 'Now we can go, the light has come.'

The announcement was received with a perceptible tremor by the only unbelieving member of our company. We had just passed the level-crossing of the Cambrian railway when Mrs. Jones directed our attention to the southern sky. While she spoke, between us and the hills, apparently two miles [3 kilometres] away, there suddenly flashed forth an enormous luminous star, an intensely brilliant white light, emitting from its whole circumference dazzling sparklets like flashing rays from a diamond.

'It may be the head light of a train?' suggested our doubting Thomas.

'No,' was Mrs. Jones's reply; 'it is too high for that.'

As though in corroboration, the star made a sudden jump towards the mountains, returning almost immediately to its old position, and then rushing at an immense speed straight for us. Then came the unmistakeable rumbling of the train approaching from the direction of Barmouth.

'I thought it was the train,' came with a sigh of relief from our unbeliever. False hope!

'No', was Mrs. Jones's confident

contradiction. 'The train light has yet to come.'

And a second light, very different in character from the first, became perceptible some distance below the star, both obviously rushing towards us. As the train drew near the 'star' disappeared. With a rush and a roar the train was past. But before our Thomas's sigh of thanks at the disappearance of the star was well out, the . . . star reappeared nearer, and if possible more brilliant than ever. Then it vanished . . .

'Wait', said Mrs. Jones. In a moment, high up on the hillside, quite two miles [3 kilometres] away from where the 'star' had been a moment previously, a 'Light' again flashed out, illuminating the heather as if bathed in brilliant sunshine. Again it vanished – only again to reappear a mile [1.6 kilometres] further north, evidently circling the valley, and in the direction for which we were bound.

And Mary Jones's lights were to assume many different forms and elude rational explanation for some time to come.

'Lighten our darkness'

What were the mysterious lights that accompanied Mary Jones's 1905 Welsh ministry? This chapter continues the bizarre tale of religious fervour and its 'UFO' connection – and considers contemporary allegations that the lights were hoaxes

MOST OF THE EYEWITNESS REPORTS we have of Mary Jones of Egryn, the 'Merionethshire Seeress' as she became known, come from local and national newspapers, and articles in the *Occult Review*. The Society for Psychical Research (SPR) produced a long and detailed report in its *Proceedings* for 1905, but conducted its investigation by postal questionnaire. However, it is hard to see what the most experienced psychical researcher, more accustomed to seances and hauntings, would have made of the following account, from the correspondent of the *Daily Mirror*. He tells of the journey back from a revival meeting:

> In the first carriage were Mrs. Jones and three ladies; in my own with me, the 'Daily Mirror' photographer, a keen-witted, hard-headed Londoner. The weirdness of that drive in semi-darkness at breakneck speed by river and mountain round deadly corners and down precipitous hills, I shall never forget. For three miles [5 kilometres] we had driven in silence, and I had given up hope. It was close on midnight, and we were nearing Barmouth when suddenly, without the faintest warning, a soft shimmering radiance flooded the road at our feet. Immediately it spread around us, and every stick and stone within twenty yards [18 metres] was visible, as if under the influence of the softest lime-light. It seemed as though some large body between earth and sky had suddenly opened and emitted a flood of light from within itself. It was a little suggestive of the bursting of a firework bomb – and yet wonderfully different. Quickly as I looked up, the light was even then fading away from the sky overhead. I seemed to see an oval mass of grey, half-open, disclosing within a kernel of white light. As I looked it closed, and everything was once again in darkness.

Who knew anything about UFOs in 1905?

The same team also witnessed another form of the phenomenon – one also described by Beriah Evans, and the Dyffryn police-constable. It seems that each night in the early part of 1905 there was a regular gathering of intrigued observers along the road by

The 'soft, shimmering radiance' that illuminated the countryside as described by the *Daily Mirror* reporter who had gone to investigate Mrs Jones and her lights. It was on the way back from a prayer meeting that the mysterious light suddenly flooded the road around them. Although it was nearly midnight the strange light picked out the detail of 'every stick and stone' within 20 yards (18 metres). The reporter and his colleague had just time to notice an oval mass of greyish light with a brilliant white kernel overhead when they were all suddenly plunged back into darkness

the chapel, all hoping for the lights to appear. The *Daily Mirror* reporter saw:

> A bar of light quite four feet [1 metre] wide, and of the most brilliant blue. It blazed out at me from the roadway, a few yards from the chapel. For half a moment it lay across the road, and then extended itself up the wall on either side. It did not rise above the walls. As I stared, fascinated, a kind of quivering radiance flashed with lightning speed from one end of the bar to the other, and the whole thing disappeared.

Meanwhile, the reporter from the *Daily Mail*, having walked several miles from Barmouth station, saw:

> A ball of fire above the roof of the chapel. It came from nowhere, and sprang into existence instantaneously. It had a steady, intense, yellow brilliance, and did not move. It seemed to me to be at twice the height of the chapel, say fifty feet [15 metres]. Suddenly it disappeared, having lasted about a minute and a half. . . . The minutes crept by, then two lights flashed out, one on each side of the chapel. They seemed about 100 yards [90 metres] apart, and about 100 feet [30 metres] above the roof of the chapel. They shone out brilliantly and steadily

for a space of 30 seconds. Then they both began to flicker while one could count ten. Then they became steady again. In the distance they looked like large and brilliant motor-car lights.

Many reports such as these could be quoted. But are there any real clues as to the nature of the phenomena described as 'stars' and 'lights'? How can we begin to track down their source? Were there real, physical lights, or were they illusions experienced by the followers of Mary Jones through the power of suggestion, when she told them that she could see lights? Were they seen only when she was present? Did they occur only in one small area? And if so, could an explanation lie in the fact that there is marshland near the chapel – might the lights have been marsh gas spontaneously igniting?

Unlikely explanations

If the phenomena had in fact occurred only around the Egryn chapel, a number of possible explanations for what was seen and reported could have been found. For example, hoaxers carrying lanterns on the hills behind the chapel would certainly have been high on the list of possibilities. So too would misapprehension of the lights of the chapel itself, or those of the scattered farmhouses in the district, or of the distant St Tudwal lighthouse. Few of the conventional sources of light encountered by UFO investigators in the 1980s would have occurred then: car lights were rare, train lights unmistakable – due to the accompanying steam engine noise

Right: the ball of fire that appeared before a reporter's startled gaze. It hovered motionless above Egryn chapel, brilliantly illuminating the roof, then abruptly disappeared. Even if this particular version of the Egryn lights could be explained away as ball lightning, Mrs Jones's other phenomena remain mysterious

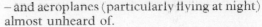

Below: the electric blue bar of light witnessed by, among others, the *Daily Mirror* reporter and a local policeman. As Mary Jones preached, this strip of light appeared across the wall by the chapel. It quivered violently – then vanished

– and aeroplanes (particularly flying at night) almost unheard of.

However, the problems in analysing the Welsh lights are not easily resolved. While the appearance of the stars and lights and, later, of other extraordinary phenomena, do seem to have been related to the presence of Mary Jones, there appears to have been no geographical limit to where they could be seen. The *Barmouth Advertiser* of 20 April 1905 reported:

This week Mrs. Mary Jones of Egryn, the 'Merionethshire Seeress' is conducting revival meetings in the Wrexham district. Some of the women present at the afternoon meeting on Monday declare that they saw a light hovering over the head of Mrs. Jones while she was speaking and praying.

At the evening meeting, as she delivered a very powerful address, and offered a most earnest prayer, the 'lights' were seen by a large number of people in the chapel. The first was a flash like lightning while she delivered the first part of her address; a second flash appeared when she began in her address to describe the 'lights' in the Egryn district, and a third flash was seen when she was praying. She said in the course of her address that the

Above: the interior of the unassuming Egryn chapel as it was in 1905. During a meeting in April many witnesses saw strange lights flash around Mary Jones's head. And on several occasions the lights hovering outside the chapel flooded it with an unearthly glow

'lights' had appeared wherever she had visited, with two exceptions, and now she knew that she had not been divinely guided to go to those places where the lights did not follow her. The visit of Mrs. Jones, followed by the lights, has created quite a sensation in the district. Wrexham (in what is now Clwyd) is on the other side of Wales from Egryn.

Two fiery arms

On 23 July 1905, about three weeks after Mrs Jones had held a mission nearby, a group of young people returning from a prayer meeting at Ynysybwl, near Ponty-pridd, Glamorgan, had a remarkable ex-perience. They told local reporters: 'There appeared in the heavens a very large and bright ball of fire. It had two brilliant arms which protruded towards the earth. Between these arms appeared lights resembling a cluster of stars, quivering with varying brightness. It lasted for ten minutes. . . .'

A doctor from Tylorstown recounted for the SPR enquiry an incident that occurred on 27 May 1905.

About 10 p.m. on Saturday night I was coming home with my wife, when she drew my attention to a bright light over the Libanus Chapel, towards the side of the mountain. It appeared as a ball of fire about the size of a cheese-plate; it was perfectly fixed. As soon as I saw it I marked its position, in order to be sure that it could not be some one with a light on the road which passes over the mountain, but its position was far enough away from the road.

Meanwhile, in April 1905, three clergymen from the Llangollen area gave the *Barmouth Advertiser* the results of their own investi-gations. The three had watched the part of the Dee Valley where Mary Jones claimed lights had appeared over the homes of those who were 'spiritually troubled'. They saw 'two large balls of fire rise from the earth and suddenly burst luridly. On the third occa-sion . . . a similar light travelling towards Vroncysyllte.' All were satisfied that, 'Some

Below right: on 23 July 1905 a group of young Methodists returning from one of Mary Jones's Glamorganshire meetings witnessed one of the more spectacular phenomena associated with her. A 'ball of fire' appeared in the sky with two brilliant 'arms' reaching to the ground. Between them was a host of twinkling stars. They watched this 'display' for about 10 minutes, then suddenly the sky returned to normal

mysterious phenomenon had appeared in their midst simultaneously with the visit of the seeress.' Together with the many other calm and responsible reports from witnesses all over Wales, it makes a solid case for a genuine mystery. Hoax, misapprehension, illusion, or natural explanations seem par-ticularly unlikely here.

Newspapers have hinted that there was a UFO connection, and the links between the revival phenomena and other well-established paranormal events seem clear enough. The following piece from the *Occult Review* hints at the scope of what is involved:

The bedroom of an exceptionally intel-ligent young woman in the neighbour-hood has been visited three times in succession by a man dressed in black, whose appearance corresponds with that of the 'Devil' seen by Mrs. Jones. This figure has delivered a message to the girl which, however, she is forbid-den to relate. In Bryncrug, a similar apparition was seen simultaneously from different standpoints. A local pro-fessional man, startled, uttered an in-voluntary prayer. Immediately, one of Mrs. Jones's mysterious 'lights' ap-peared above, a white ray darting from it which pierced the figure, which there-upon vanished. An apparition, appear-ing first as a man, then transforming itself into a large black dog, was seen at Abergynolwyn, a mining centre not far distant.

A fading star

While mysterious lights flashed and hovered around Mary Jones, other strange events were reported in the Egryn area. Coincidence? Or were all the phenomena projections from Mrs Jones?

THE LIGHTS ASSOCIATED with Mary Jones in 1905 were not the first to be seen in the north-western part of Wales. The *Barmouth Advertiser* found this account in a geography of Wales published in about 1800:

> 'Tis creditably reported that in the year 1692 a fiery exhalation was seen to cross the sea, and set fire to the ricks of hay, corn and barns near Harlech, and to infect the grass, but was not mischievous to men, though they were in the midst of it. It proceeded in the night from the same place for some months, commonly on Saturdays or Sundays. The only remedy to extinguish or drive it away was to sound horns or trumpets, or to discharge guns.

The Reverend Fryer, who conducted the enquiry for the Society for Psychical Research (SPR), found similar – though less dramatic – reports of blue or white lights in 1869, 1875 and 1877, at points along the Cambrian coast.

Perhaps if the contemporary investigations into the lights had been more thorough, we might now be able to say what really happened in 1905. The investigations that did take place were far from adequate, though the problems that the phenomena presented were many. How do you catch, or

Above: Welsh converts during the revival of 1904 to 1905 queue to be baptised

Below: Denbigh Asylum, last earthly home of some who suffered religious mania

measure, or analyse a flying light? As it is, we can only consider how trustworthy the witnesses were, and look for common features in their reports.

The *Daily Mail* sent a Mr Redwood, the son of a famous scientist, to investigate. He set up some sort of 'instruments capable of being influenced by any extraordinary electrical condition of the atmosphere', about a mile (1.6 kilometres) from the Egryn chapel. Unfortunately, despite several hours' waiting in heavy rain, he recorded no positive results save for a sudden onslaught by two other observers who, believing the light from his lantern to be miraculous, rushed up and took a photograph of it. But a local man had warned him before his experiment: 'Ah, you won't see the light tonight, for Mrs Mary Jones has gone away.'

Of the British newspapers, only the *Manchester Guardian* seems to have sent someone to talk to the actual witnesses to find out what was really happening. The article, credited to 'A visitor', appeared on 14 February 1905 and was entitled 'Fire without and within'. After a discussion of the place of the lights in the current religious revival, it concluded:

> While everybody speaks of Mrs. Jones with great respect, a good many of her neighbours smile when the lights are mentioned. They have not seen them, though they are always sweeping the heavens with their eyes. One man saw two arc-like lights one night which were neither stars nor lamp-lights but may, he thinks, have been produced in some oblique way by the rays of the moon. 'I have often seen Mrs. Jones driving to Revival meetings,' said the same man, 'but I have never seen any lights attending her. . . .'

A woman who thoroughly believes in the lights says she saw a large star one evening as she was going into Chapel. 'Nearly as big as the moon – well, not

The Times had reported: 'Ten patients suffering from religious mania are already in the Joint Counties Asylum at Denbigh. One or two show signs of improvement, but the general condition of the others is stated to be very bad.'

Paranormal events are always being reported, regardless of revivals, evangelists, or enquiring journalists. Generally, only a small proportion of those people who have such experiences make them public, and it must be assumed that in 1905 a higher proportion than usual were persuaded, due to press interest and revival enthusiasm, to do so. Many other accounts of unusual events did reach investigators. The SPR enquiry discovered a clergyman who heard a choir of voices singing a previously undocumented Welsh hymn in the middle of a deserted hillside. Various men in Montgomeryshire heard bells in a church service, the sound of singing along an empty road, and an unexplained thunderclap. A minister from Maesteg told of how a young parishioner suddenly 'knew', while praying in church, of the death of his absent father. An unnamed woman, probably in early 1905, is rumoured to have seen a column of fire below which appeared the Egryn chapel, apparently in mid-flight; it later turned into an 'eye', split into two parts, fell, and re-formed

quite so big – and a bluish colour.' It had disappeared when she came out of the chapel two hours later. . . .

Taking the existence of the 'lights' to be admitted – and there seems to be abundant evidence – it may be hoped that some competent enquiry will be directed as to their cause. . . . As against the purely physical character of the 'lights', they are said at the same time to be visible to some and invisible to others.

Certainly, local feelings about the lights did seem to be mixed, and some who had at first been enthusiastic about the phenomena later saw them as a liability, and an embarrassment bringing ridicule upon local people. The *Cambrian News*, published in Aberystwyth, came to be of this opinion. On 24 February 1905, after reporting lights at Tre'rddol, it commented:

When a person sees flashing lights he may take it for granted that he has jim-jams. Jim-jams are really dangerous, and when he hears knockings as well he is in a fair way to find himself locked up in a padded room. . . .

Over the next few weeks it continued with its criticism, crowning its efforts in verse:

If these things you see and hear,
Sometimes distant, sometimes near
Don't you seek to reconcile 'em,
They'll do that in the Asylum!

It must be admitted that on 10 January 1905

Above: during Mrs Jones's ministry it was rumoured that an unnamed woman had a vision of a flying Egryn chapel surrounded by a pillar of fire. This was only one of the many reported paranormal events associated with the Welsh revival

Right: St Elmo's fire, a natural phenomenon akin to that of ball lightning – one of the alternative explanations to Mrs Jones's lights

Below: St Tudwal's lighthouse, whose flashing light could have been taken as miraculous

into what appeared to be the shape of a man.

A similar experience was had by 'an aged Welsh bard of some repute', who had been unable 'to forgo the temptations of the tavern'. He found himself in a 'strange land', being threatened by 'ravening beasts'. Rescued by a mysterious figure from this predicament, he said: 'I realised I had seen my Saviour.' He gave up drinking, took up missionary work during the revival, and 'influenced for good many of his old boon companions'.

Though the visions of the converts happened in the same country as the lights, amid the same religious fervour (and were reported in the same magazines and newspapers), they are probably entirely different phenomena, although no one today can be sure.

A matter of history

There are many problems to be overcome in attempting any assessment of the lights associated with Mary Jones. It is now many years since the phenomena occurred. Though there are many cases, most are undated, and those reported to the SPR are often anonymous; it is difficult to assess their worth. We know little of weather conditions and other vital factors at the times the lights were seen. Faced with possible explanations as varied as sightings of Venus, of St Elmo's fire, of marsh gas, ball lightning, phosphorescence, fireflies, and the lights of St Tudwal's lighthouse, it is impossible to investigate further. Any of these might or might not have caused any particular incident. A holiday the author took at Tal-y-Bont (a village near Egryn) revealed few local memories of either Mrs Jones or her phenomena. Local explanations related to 'men carrying lanterns in the fields' and 'moonlight shining on broken glass'.

The key to any objective assessment of the phenomena lies in the independent testimony from journalists and clergymen. This does seem strong enough to support the view that genuinely paranormal events did take place. Most of them took the form of varying shapes of bright white or coloured light, behaving in an entirely mysterious manner. That the lights were seen, and that they were seen to move in an apparently purposeful manner, appears certain. As *The Guardian* said of them, 'There seems to be abundant evidence.'

So, if the lights, with their paranormal behaviour, did occur, or were seen to occur, how and why did they do so? Where did they come from, what directed their behaviour, and where did they go?

There are no firm answers to these questions, but perhaps the best clue lies in what the lights, by their appearance and behaviour, achieved. That was, simply, Mrs Jones's own ambitions: to be the 'accepted medium for the spreading of the Revival in Merionethshire', and to run a successful mission in her own local chapel. The lights

were the means of her fame, and the basis of the remarkable extent of her missionary work. She believed her faith created the lights and this gave her the power to convert.

But if the evidence does argue for the physical, though paranormal, reality of the lights, then there seem to be only two possible explanations. Either God was demonstrating his power to convert sinners – or some equally extraordinary, but more natural, factor was responsible. In short, the production of visible, controllable phenomena, perhaps constructed of some form of electrical energy, by an act of conscious or unconscious will; and there we find ourselves in the area of poltergeists (which seem to occur in the vicinity of the emotionally troubled), and the physical phenomena of Spiritualism.

Whether or not the will of Mary Jones could conjure up lights that would do her bidding, we are unlikely ever to know. Although she continued her mission until the revival finally lost its force in 1906, there is no known report of the lights after July 1905.

Of Mary Jones's later life we know little, but it seems she never found domestic happiness. Her husband – of whom we know nothing – died in 1909, and both her daughter and her son died young. She continued to teach at Egryn chapel Sunday school, and occasionally took part in prayer meetings. She lived on alone, near the chapel, until her death in 1936, and she was buried in the Horeb cemetery at Dyffryn, where the grave can still be seen. After her hard life, with its brief, yet remarkable, interlude of fame, perhaps it is as well that her achievements are not entirely forgotten.

Right: Mary Jones's tombstone in the Horeb cemetery at Dyffryn in north Wales. She died lonely and forgotten in 1936. The lights had long since abandoned her

As UFO sightings increase so, allegedly, does the harassment of the witnesses – by the sinister Men In Black. HILARY EVANS discusses these frightening and bizarre encounters

'I WENT INTO THE FANTASTIC and came up with the answer,' declared Albert Bender, director of the International Flying Saucer Bureau, an amateur UFO organisation based in Connecticut, USA. 'I know what the saucers are.' Unfortunately, the rest of the world is still none the wiser – for Bender was prevented from passing on his discovery to the world by three sinister visitors: three men dressed in black, known as 'the silencers'.

It had been Bender's intention to publish his momentous findings in his own journal, *Space Review*. But before committing himself finally, he felt he ought to try his ideas out on a colleague. He mailed his report – and a few days later, the men came.

Bender was lying down in his bedroom, having been overtaken by a spell of dizziness, when he noticed 'three shadowy figures in the room. The figures became clearer. All of them were dressed in black clothes. They looked like clergymen, but wore hats similar to Homburg style. The faces were not clearly discernible, for the hats partly hid and shaded them. Feelings of fear left me. . . . The eyes of all three figures suddenly lit up like flashlight bulbs, and all these were focussed upon me. They seemed to burn into my very soul as the pains above my eyes

Above: most accounts of MIBS describe them as wearing conventional black suits, white shirts and black ties. Often they are said to look strangely uncomfortable as if unused to wearing such clothes. The clothes themselves seem brand-new – yet oddly old-fashioned

Right: the MIBS have a surreal quality, like people in a nightmare. Even their cars are disconcertingly new – smelling of 'new leather' – yet the models are dated and the number plates, when checked, are frequently discovered never to have been issued

became almost unbearable. It was then I sensed that they were conveying a message to me by telepathy.'

His visitors confirmed that Bender was right in his speculations as to the true nature of UFOS – one of them was carrying Bender's report – and provided additional information. This so terrified him that he was only too willing to go along with their demand that he close down his organisation and cease publication of his journal. He was instructed not to tell the truth to anyone 'on his honour as an American citizen'.

Did Bender expect anyone to believe his story? His friends and colleagues were baffled by it – one of them, Gray Barker, published a sensational book, *They knew too much about flying saucers*, and Bender himself supplied an even stranger account in his *Flying saucers and the three men* some years later, in response to persistent demands for an explanation from former colleagues. He told an extraordinary story involving extra-terrestrial spaceships with bases in Antarctica that reads like the most far-fetched contactee dreamstuff; it has been suggested that the implausibility of Bender's story is

Who are t

designed to throw serious UFO investigators off the track.

Believable or not, Bender's original account of the visit of the three strangers is of crucial interest to UFO investigators. For the story has been paralleled by many similar reports, frequently from people unlikely to have so much as heard of Bender and his experiences. UFO percipients and investigators are equally liable to be visited by men in black (MIBs); and, although the majority of reports are from the United States, similar claims have come from Sweden and Italy, Britain and Mexico. And like the UFO phenomenon, MIBs span three decades, and may well have had precursors in earlier centuries.

Like Bender's story, most of the later reports not only contain implausible details, but are also inherently illogical; in virtually every case, there seems on the face of it more reason to disbelieve than to believe. But this does not eliminate the mystery – it simply requires us to study it in a different light. For, whether or not these things actually happened, the fact remains that they were reported; and why should so many people,

independently and often reluctantly, report these strange and sinister visitations? And why is it that these accounts are so similar, echoing and in turn helping to confirm a persistent pattern that, if nothing else, is one of the most powerful folk myths of our time?

The archetypal MIB report runs something like this: shortly after a UFO sighting, the subject – he may be a witness, he may be an investigator on the case – receives a visit. Often it occurs so soon after the incident itself that no official report or media publication has taken place: in short, the visitors should not, by any normal channels, have

gained access to the information they clearly possess – names, addresses, details of the incident and about the people involved.

The victim is nearly always alone at the time of the visit, usually in his own home. His visitors, usually three in number, arrive in a large black car. In America it is most often a prestigious Cadillac, but seldom a recent model. At the same time, though old in date, it is likely to be new and immaculate in appearance and condition, inside and out, even having that unmistakable 'new car' smell. If the subject notes the registration number and checks it, it is invariably found to be a non-existent number.

The visitors themselves are almost always men: only very rarely is one a woman, and never more than one. In appearance they conform pretty closely to the stereotyped image of a CIA or secret service man. They wear dark suits, dark hats, dark ties, dark shoes and socks, but white shirts: witnesses very often remark on their clean, immaculate turn-out – all the clothes looking as though just purchased.

The visitors' faces are frequently described as vaguely foreign, most often 'oriental': slant eyes have been specified in many accounts. If not dark skinned, the men are likely to be very heavily tanned. Sometimes there are bizarre touches; in the case of Dr Hopkins, which we shall look at more closely later, the man in black appeared to be wearing bright lipstick! The MIBs are generally unsmiling and expressionless, their

Right: Albert Bender, American UFO investigator, with one of his many representations of a UFO landing. Bender is an eccentric occult and horror enthusiast who claims that he was prevented from making public his insights into the nature of UFOs by the threats of three MIBs

e Men In Black?

Agents of the dark

Rarely – if ever – do the threats of the mysterious men in black come to anything. So what is the purpose behind their visits?

IN SEPTEMBER 1976 Dr Herbert Hopkins, a 58-year-old doctor and hypnotist, was acting as consultant on an alleged UFO teleportation case in Maine, USA. One evening, when his wife and children had gone out leaving him alone, the telephone rang and a man identifying himself as vice-president of the New Jersey UFO Research Organisation asked if he might visit Dr Hopkins to discuss the case. Dr Hopkins agreed – at the time it seemed the natural thing to do. He went to the back door to switch on the light so that his visitor could find his way from the parking lot, and saw the man already climbing the porch steps. 'I saw no car, and even if he did have a car, he could not have possibly gotten to my house that quickly from *any* phone,' he later commented in astonishment.

But at the time Dr Hopkins felt no particular surprise as he admitted his visitor. The man was dressed in a black suit, with black hat, tie and shoes, and a white shirt: 'I thought, he looks like an undertaker.' His clothes were immaculate: suit unwrinkled, trousers sharply creased. When he took off his hat he revealed himself as completely hairless, not only bald but without eyebrows or eyelashes. His skin was dead white, his lips bright red: in the course of their conversation he brushed his lips with his grey suede gloves, and the doctor was astonished to see that his lips were smeared and the gloves stained with lipstick!

Visitor from another dimension?

It was only afterwards, however, that Dr Hopkins reflected on the strangeness of his visitor's appearance and behaviour. At the time he sat discussing the case in a normal manner. When he had given his account, his visitor stated that his host had two coins in his pocket, which was indeed the case. He asked the doctor to put one of the coins in his hand: he did so. The stranger asked Dr Hopkins to watch the coin, not himself: as he watched, the coin seemed to go out of focus, and then gradually vanished. 'Neither you nor anyone else on this plane will ever see that coin again,' the visitor told him.

After talking a little while longer on UFO topics, Dr Hopkins noticed that the visitor's

An MIB visited Dr Herbert Hopkins and told him to discontinue his investigations into an alleged UFO teleportation case on which he was working at the time. Taking a coin from Dr Hopkins, the MIB made it disappear – remarking that 'Neither you nor anyone else on this plane will ever see that coin again'

speech was slowing down. The man rose unsteadily to his feet and said, very slowly, 'My energy is running low – must go now – goodbye.' He walked falteringly to the door, and descended the outside steps uncertainly, one at a time. Dr Hopkins saw a bright light shining in the driveway, bluish-white and distinctly brighter than a normal car lamp; at the time, however, he assumed it must be the stranger's car although he neither saw nor heard it.

Later, When Dr Hopkins's family had

returned, they examined the driveway and found marks that could not have been made by a car because they were in the centre of the driveway, where the wheels could not have been. By next day, although the driveway had not been used in the meantime, the marks had vanished.

Dr Hopkins was very much shaken by his visit, particularly when he reflected on the extraordinary character of the stranger's conduct. Not surprisingly, he was so scared that he willingly complied with his visitor's instruction to erase the tapes of the hypnotic sessions he was conducting with regard to his current case, and to have nothing further to do with the case.

Curious incidents continued to occur both in Dr Hopkins's household and in that of his eldest son. He presumed that there was some link with the extraordinary visit, but he never heard from his visitor again. As for the New Jersey UFO Research Organisation, no such institution exists.

Dr Hopkins's account is probably the most detailed we have of an MIB visit, and confronts us with the problem at its most bizarre. First we must ask ourselves if a trained and respected doctor would invent so strange a tale, and if so, with what conceivable motive? Alternatively, could the entire episode have been a delusion, despite the tracks seen by other members of his family? Could the truth lie somewhere between reality and imagination: that is to say, could there have been a real visitor, albeit an impostor making a false identity claim, visiting the doctor for some unknown reason of his own, and somehow acting as a trigger for the doctor to invent a whole set of weird features that to a third party might have had some quite natural explanation?

Frightening aftermath

What seems the *least* likely explanation is that the whole incident took place in the doctor's imagination. When his wife and children came home, they found him severely shaken, with the house lights blazing, seated at a table on which lay a gun. They confirmed the marks on the driveway, and a

The odd couple

On 24 September 1976 – only a few days after Dr Hopkins's terrifying visit from an MIB – his daughter-in-law Maureen received a telephone call from a man who claimed to know her husband John, and asked if he and a companion could come and visit them.

John met the man at a local fast-food

restaurant, and brought him home with his companion, a woman. Both appeared to be in their mid-thirties; they wore curiously old-fashioned clothes. The woman looked particularly odd: her breasts were set very low, and when she stood up, it seemed that there was something wrong with the way that her legs joined onto her hips. Both strangers walked with very short steps, leaning forward as though frightened of falling.

They accepted Coca-Colas, but did not so much as taste them. The strangers sat awkwardly together on a sofa while the man asked a number of detailed personal questions: Did John and Maureen watch television much? What did they read? And what did they talk about? All the while, the man was pawing and fondling his female companion, asking John if this was all right and whether he was doing it correctly.

John left the room for a moment, and the man tried to persuade Maureen to sit next to him on the couch. He also asked her 'how she was made' – and whether she had any nude photographs of herself.

Shortly afterwards, the woman stood up, and announced that she wanted to leave. The man also stood, but made no move to go. He was between the woman and the door, and it seemed that the only way she could get to the door was by walking in a straight line, directly through him. Finally the woman turned to John and asked, 'Please move him; I can't move him myself.' Then, suddenly, the man left, followed by the woman, both walking in straight lines. They did not even say goodbye.

Towards the end of Dr Hopkins's MIB visit, he noticed that the man's speech and movements seemed to be slowing down. The MIB got up unsteadily and left, walking very shakily; Dr Hopkins watched him walk down the front steps of his house and into the driveway, and saw a bright, bluish-white light – far too intense for car headlights – but failed to see, or hear, anything else as the stranger departed

series of disturbances on the telephone that seemed to commence immediately after the visit. So it would seem that some real event occurred, although its nature remains mystifyingly uncertain.

The concrete nature of the phenomenon was accepted by the United States Air Force, who were concerned that persons passing themselves off as USAF personnel should be visiting UFO witnesses. In February 1967 Colonel George P. Freeman, Pentagon spokesman for the USAF's Project Blue Book, told UFO investigator John Keel in the course of an interview:

'Mysterious men dressed in Air Force uniforms or bearing impressive credentials from government agencies have been "silencing" UFO witnesses. We have checked a number of these cases, and these men are not connected with the Air Force in any way. We haven't been able to find out anything about these men. By posing as Air Force officers and government agents they are committing a federal offence. We would sure like to catch one. Unfortunately the trail is always too cold by the time we hear about these cases. But we're still trying.'

A question remains: were the impostors referred to by Colonel Freeman and Dr Hopkins's strange visitor similar in kind? UFO sightings, like sensational crimes, attract a number of mentally unstable persons, who are quite capable of posing as authorised officials in order to gain access to the witnesses; it is likely that some supposed MIBS are simply pseudo-investigators of this sort.

One curious recurrent feature of MIB reports is the ineptitude of the visitors. Time and again they are described as incompetent: if they *are* impersonating human beings, they don't do it very well; they arouse their

David Tansley, a UFO theorist who has suggested that MIBs are some kind of demonic psychic entity

victim's suspicions by improbable behaviour, by the way they look or talk, by their ignorance as much as by their knowledge. Of course it could be that the only ones who are spotted as impostors are those who are not good at their job: and so there may be many more MIB cases that we never learn about simply because the visitors successfully convince their victims that there is nothing suspicious about the visit, or that they will do best to keep quiet about it.

A feature of a great many MIB visits is the instruction to the witness not to say anything about the visit, and to cease all activity concerning the case: clearly, we know of these cases only because such instructions have been disobeyed. Curiously, however, no terrible retribution follows, although violence is frequently threatened if the witness does not comply with instructions. Canadian UFO witness Carmen Cuneo, in 1976, was told by a mysterious visitor to stop repeating his story and going further into his case, or he would be visited by three men in black. 'I said, "What's that supposed to mean?" "Well," he said, "I could make it hot for you . . . It might cost you certain injury."' A year earlier, Mexican witness Carlos de Los Santos was stopped on his way to a television interview by not one but two large black limousines, and one of the occupants – dressed in a black suit and 'Scandinavian' in appearance – told him, 'Look, boy, if you value your life and your family's too, don't talk any more about this sighting of yours.'

However, there is no reliable instance of such threats ever having been carried out, though a good many witnesses have defied their warnings. Indeed, sinister though the MIBs may be, they are notable for the lack of violence associated with them: the worst that can be said of them is that they harass the witnesses with their untimely visits and telephone calls, or simply disturb them with their very presence.

Threats of violence

While for the victim it is just as well that the threats of violence are not followed through, this is for the investigator one more disconcerting aspect of the phenomenon. For violence, if it resulted in physical action, would at least help to establish the reality of the phenomenon. For it remains a fact that most of the evidence is purely hearsay in character, and not often of the highest quality: cases as well-attested as those of Mr Richardson and Dr Hopkins are unfortunately in the minority. There is a dismaying lack of precision about too many of the reports. Popular American writer Brad Steiger alleges that '*hundreds* of ufologists, contactees and chance percipients of UFOs claimed to have been visited by ominous strangers – usually three, usually dressed in black'; but he cites only a few anecdotal instances. Similarly, John Keel, an expert on unexplained phenomena, claims 'on a number of occasions I actually saw the phantom Cadillacs as advertised, complete with sinister-looking Oriental-like passengers in black suits', but for a trained reporter he shows a curious reluctance to pursue these sightings or to give us chapter and verse in such an important matter. Such loose assertions are valueless as evidence: all they do is contribute to the myth.

And so we come back once again to the MIB myth, and the possibility that there is nothing more to the phenomenon than the myth itself. Can we not write off the whole business as delusion, the creation of imaginative folk whose personal obsessions take on this particular shape because it reflects one or other of the prevalent cultural preoccupations of our time? At one extreme we find contactee Woodrow Derenberger insisting that the 'two men dressed entirely in black' who tried to silence him were emissaries of the Mafia: at the other, theorist David Tansley suggests that they are psychic entities, representatives of the dark forces, seeking to prevent the spread of true knowledge. More matter-of-factly Dominick

Lucchesi, one of Albert Bender's friends, held that they emanated from some unknown civilisation, possibly underground, in a remote area of Earth – the Amazon, the Gobi Desert or the Himalayas.

But there is one feature that is common to virtually all MIB reports, that any theory must account for, and that perhaps contains the key to the problem. This is the possession, by the MIBs, of information that they should not have been able to come by – information that was restricted, not released to the press, known perhaps to a few investigators and officials but not to the public, and

A Mexican UFO witness, Carlos de los Santos, was stopped by MIBs travelling in two large black limousines on his way to a television interview about his UFO sighting. The MIBs warned him to keep silent, and he cancelled the interview. Two weeks later, however, he changed his mind and made the broadcast – and not a word was heard from the MIBs, despite their threats

sometimes not even to them. The one person who *does* possess that knowledge is the person visited. In other words, the MIBs and their victim share knowledge that perhaps nobody else possesses. Add to this the fact that in almost every case the MIBs appear to the witness when he or she is alone – in Dr Hopkins's case, for example, the visitor took care to call when the wife and children were away from home, and established this fact by telephone beforehand. The implication has to be that some kind of paranormal link connects the MIBs and the persons they visit.

Truth – or paranoia?
To this must be added other features of the phenomenon that are not easily reconciled with everyday reality. These notorious black cars, for instance: where are they, when they are not visiting witnesses? Where are they garaged, serviced? Do they never get involved in breakdowns or accidents? Can it be that they materialise from some other plane of existence when they are needed?

These are only a few of the questions raised by the MIB phenomenon. What complicates the matter is that MIB cases lie along a continuous spectrum ranging from the easily believable to the totally incredible. At one extreme are visits during which nothing really bizarre occurs, the only anomalous feature being, perhaps, that the visitor makes a false identity claim, or has unaccountable access to private information. But at the other extreme are cases in which the only explanation would seem to be that the witness has succumbed to paranoia. In *The truth about the men in black*, UFO investigator Ramona Clark tells of an unnamed investigator who was confronted by three MIBs on 3 July 1969. 'On the window of the car in which they were riding was the symbol connected with them and their visitations. This symbol had a profound psychological impact upon this man. I have never encountered such absolute fear in a human being.'

That first meeting was followed by continual harassment. There were mysterious telephone calls; the man's house was searched. He began to hear voices and see strange shapes. 'Black Cadillacs roamed the street in front of his home, and followed him everywhere he went. Once he and his family were almost forced into an accident by an oncoming Cadillac. Nightmares concerning MIBs plagued his sleep. It became impossible for him to rest, his work suffered and he was scared of losing his job.'

Was it all in his mind? One is tempted to think so. But a friend confirmed that, while they talked, there was a strange-looking man walking back and forth in front of the house. The man was tall, seemed about 55 years old – and was dressed entirely in black.

The long shadow of fear

Men in black excited a great deal of attention when they began to threaten UFO witnesses in the 1950s. But the powerful symbol of the sinister black-clad figure is centuries old

UFO PERCIPIENTS AND INVESTIGATORS are by no means the only people to receive visits from men in black. Researchers Kevin and Sue McClure, investigating the North Wales religious revival of 1905, found accounts that bear at least a *prima facie* similarity to the current MIB phenomenon:

> In the neighbourhood dwells an exceptionally intelligent young woman of the peasant class, whose bedroom has been visited three nights in succession at midnight by a man dressed in black. This figure has delivered a message to the girl which, however, she is forbidden to relate.

The young woman in question, farmer's wife-turned-preacher Mary Jones – one of the leading figures of the revival – was well known for the mysterious lights that appeared as she pursued her mission. On one occasion when she encountered her sinister visitor at night, Mary was 'rescued' by one of her lights, which darted a white ray at the apparition. The MIB promptly vanished.

It all sounds like the wildest fantasy – except that there is substantial evidence for some of the phenomena reported, many of which were seen by several independent witnesses, some of them avowedly sceptical. Does this mean that the MIBs *really* existed, *really* appeared in the bedroom of that 'intelligent young woman of the peasant class'? What we are learning about the current wave of MIBs may help us to understand similar cases reported in earlier periods.

Men in black turn up, in one form or another, in the folklore of every country, and periodically they emerge from legend

Above: Montague Summers (1880–1948), a writer who found a number of historical MIB cases – years before the first modern, UFO-related MIB encounter in 1953

Below: the Last Judgement, by Fra Angelico (c.1400–1455): the damned (right) are being dragged off to hell by black demons. Some modern writers have gone as far as to suggest an identification between these sinister figures and MIBs

into everyday life. On 2 June 1603, a young country lad confessed before a court in south-west France to several acts of werewolfery, culminating in kidnapping and eating a child. He stated that he was acting under the orders of the Lord of the Forest, to whom he was bond-slave. The Lord of the Forest he described as a tall dark man, dressed all in black, and riding a black horse.

Under the cover of darkness . . .

Montague Summers, who reports the case in his book *The werewolf* (1933), has no hesitation in identifying this and all other MIBs with the Devil of Christian teaching, and this continues to be a widespread interpretation: even today there are theorists who claim that UFOs are diabolical in origin, and the MIBs consequently must be Satan's agents. In the parts of the world where the prevailing religious doctrine presupposes two warring factions of good and evil, good is equated with light and evil with darkness, the agents of good tend to be blond and dressed in white, while the agents of evil have dark hair and are dressed in black. Other connotations follow naturally. Under cover of darkness, all kinds of tricks can be carried out and crimes committed. Darkness is also associated with winter, and so with death: in almost all parts of the world, death rites and customs are associated with the colour black.

So, whatever his specific role, the MIB is a distinctly sinister figure. He is a trickster, not working openly; he stands for lies rather than truth, death rather than life.

Because of the obviously symbolic elements involved, many theorists speculate that MIBs are not flesh-and-blood creatures at all, but mental constructs projected from the imagination of the percipient, and taking on a form that blends traditional legend with contemporary imagery. But it can't be quite that simple: too many of the accounts show evidence of relating to physical creatures moving in the real, physical world.

To those who report MIB encounters, there are several possible origins. At his most concrete, the MIB is supposed to be the representative of an official department; sometimes as straightforward and above-board as the Air Force, sometimes a more covert organisation such as the CIA or FBI. The average American, in particular, seems

Below: a representation of the demon god Kal Bahairab from the Hanuman Doka temple in Nepal. The god was always shown with a hideous face, four arms and – significantly – black skin. Human beings were, in former times, sacrificed to it to satisfy its lust for blood

religious and scientific institutions. They – the MIB – have a very long background and history that stretches back for centuries, indicating a massive build-up of concentration to where it is today.

MIBs are often reported as dark skinned, as having either defective command of English, or conversely an over-precise, over-meticulous way of speaking that suggests that they are not speaking a tongue natural to them. Mary Hyre, a West Virginia journalist, noted that a strange visitor picked up a ball-point pen from her desk and examined it with amazement, as if he had never seen anything like it before. And UFO percipient Mrs Ralph Butler, who received a visit from a man who claimed to be an Air Force major, was astonished to find that he was so unfamiliar with American food that he had to be shown how to eat it. The implication is that they are foreigners, an attitude encouraged by American xenophobia. Curiously, though, no witness appears to have suggested that the MIBS are of Russian origin: where specific details are mentioned, it is always implied that they are vaguely 'oriental'. Slanting eyes are frequently reported; the deadpan faces suggest the inscrutable Asiatic; sometimes heads are totally bald. (By linking 'the yellow peril' with the 'man in black', of course, it is possible to frighten oneself with two bogey-men for the price of one!)

Although witnesses rarely state openly that they believe their visitors to come from beyond Earth, this is often clearly implied. Bender's three men were clearly of alien origin. Other MIBs have displayed behaviour traits that seem to suggest that they are able to function only for a limited time-span: after a while they insist that they have to leave, or take pills, or ask for water, and sometimes show signs of losing strength.

A further possibility remains: that the MIBS are neither flesh-and-blood (even extra-terrestrial flesh-and-blood) on the one hand, nor pure hallucination/illusion on the other, but something in between. The entities encountered in a recent French case seem to have existed, if existed is the word, on some alternative plane of being.

far from convinced that investigative bodies such as the CIA are necessarily working in the public interest, and the same attitude of mind as has evolved the conspiracy theories about UFOs, that a gigantic cover-up is being mounted by the government, suggests that the MIBS are part of this operation, their sole object being to conceal the facts by silencing witnesses and purloining photographs and other evidence.

The fact that the identities of a great many MIBS have been checked, and they have invariably been found not to be the persons they purport to be, lends strength to this suspicion, which can amount to virtual paranoia. Thus in 1970 an American theorist, Tony Kimery, wrote in all seriousness:

The mysterious MIB and the entire collection of their thugs, henchmen, and highly trained intelligence officers, are a big part of the complex UFO phenomena which is in turn part of another big and complex phenomena (*sic*). It is known that projects by them are now under way for the complete control of . . . political, financial,

Below: Richard Baxter, a 17th-century writer, who recounted the tale of a London woman of the time – a 'pious, credible woman' – who was encouraged to hang herself by the Devil in the shape of a big black man. The archetype of black as a symbol of evil reappears in the MIB myth

Abduction and threats

The alleged abduction, in December 1979, of Franck Fontaine for seven days on board a UFO was one of the rare French cases to have attracted worldwide attention. The abduction itself was of course the central event of the case, but it was only the start of a series of incidents: one of these, involving MIBS, concerned another member of the trio, Jean-Pierre Prévost, who told this story:

'The night of Friday the seventh to Saturday the eighth of December 1979, Franck, Salomon and I had sat up talking for a long time, and went to bed sometime around 5 to 5.30 in the morning. At 7 there was a ring at the door: Salomon and Franck didn't hear it, so I went to open the door. I found myself in the presence of three fellows. One was of average height, very well dressed in dark green, almost black, black tie, white shirt, and waistcoat to match his suit; he had a fringe of beard, black like his hair, and a moustache. His general appearance was pretty good. The others were bigger than him, taller and more heavily built.

'What follows, I haven't told the police – I reported the visit itself to them – because we've already had enough of being taken for crackpots! But these two types, with the bearded man, didn't really exist, that I'm certain of! In the first place, they had no sight. That's hard to explain: they fixed me with their eyes, but those eyes were nothing but a white mass, all over. They were terrifying!

'The bearded fellow asked me, Are you one of the three?, by which obviously he meant, was I one of the three people concerned in the Cergy-Pontoise case? I said yes, and he went on, Good, in that case, you can pass the word to your companions: you've already said too much. An accident will happen to you. And if you say any more, it will be more serious than that . . .

'And with that they vanished; but how, that's something I can't begin to explain. They didn't take the lift, I'd have heard it if they did; and even more so if they'd used the stairs, the door makes a deafening row! I went to the window that overlooks the parking lot. I can tell you definitely that all night, at least until 5 a.m. or later, we'd noticed a Ford Capri in metallic green standing beneath our window, a Ford that we didn't recognise. Well, when I looked down, there was this Ford, just starting up. How had they managed to get to it without using the stairs or the lift? Complete mystery.

'I woke up Franck and Salomon and we went to the police, without giving them the unbelievable details about the two toughs. The police said, So long as they didn't actually attack or wound you, there's nothing we can do, so get back home. And that was that.'

Forces of evil
Jean-Pierre told investigators that he had seen the three men on several subsequent occasions. Generally, it was simply a matter of seeing them across the street or at a market, but on one occasion he received another warning while he was in a tobacco store buying cigarettes, telling him to keep quiet about their experiences and making threats. Subsequently, under hypnosis, Jean-Pierre indicated that the entities were not extra-terrestrials but *intra*-terrestrials, forces of evil from inside the Earth. He also added – intriguingly – that the bearded man had been real but that his two henchmen had been unreal.

Cases such as this are made baffling by their inconsequentiality. But one thing

Salomon N'Diaye, Jean-Pierre Prévost and Franck Fontaine (above, left to right) were involved in a famous case of alleged abduction by the UFO shown in the sketch (inset). Prévost was later the victim of a threatening visit from MIBS

seems certain: just as the MIB visits seem to originate from some psychic or mental link between the MIBs and the witness, so the consequences of the visit depend less on the MIBs than on the attitude adopted by the witness. If he takes the MIBs at their face value, if he believes their threats, he is liable to find himself heading for a breakdown: paranoia may develop, and he may believe himself followed everywhere, harassed by paranormal happenings such as strange telephone calls and poltergeist phenomena. It is even possible that these second-stage phenomena are genuine as far as the victim himself is concerned: they are manifestations of his fears – but none the less real for that – and will not disappear until he capitulates and gives up his UFO studies, if he is an investigator, or keeps quiet about his experiences if he is a witness.

If, on the other hand, he braves the matter out – if he refuses to abandon his investigation, continues to tell the world of his experiences – it seems the MIBs are powerless against him. Carlos de los Santos, stopped on his way to a television interview by a gang of tough, threatening characters, was momentarily scared; he turned his car round, went home and cancelled the interview. But a friend reassured him and persuaded him not to let himself be intimidated: a fortnight later he gave the interview – and there wasn't a squeak from the MIBs!

The MIB phenomenon is clearly worth studying carefully. Whatever the nature of the MIBs – whether they are wholly illusory, or whether there is a measure of reality in them – they exert a great deal of power over the minds of their victims. The better we understand them, the more we may learn about how such power may be deployed. And, if for no other reason, the MIB phenomenon is important because it gives the sociologist a chance to study a legend in the making. The sinister MIB masquerade provides us with contemporary phenomena that rank with the witch, the vampire and the werewolf of times past.

The farmer and the cosmonauts

Cousins of the human race dwell in the Pleiades star cluster – and a Swiss farmer is their confidant on Earth. PETER BROOKESMITH analyses his claims, and the remarkably detailed photographs that back them up

EARLY ONE JANUARY AFTERNOON in 1975, a Swiss farmer, Billy Meier, was out walking near his home at Hinwel, in Zürich canton. He looked across the empty road to the meadow opposite and reflected on how remote this stretch of countryside was. Just then, however, he realised that he was not alone: a peculiar hum filled the air. He looked up and saw a classic UFO – a silver disc-shaped craft – circling slowly above him.

By unusual good fortune Billy Meier was carrying a camera. He managed to take a number of pictures of the craft before it 'swooped down' and landed about 300 feet (100 metres) away from him. He judged it to be about 23 feet (7 metres) in diameter. He began to run towards it, but was stopped by 'an unknown force' some 150 feet (50 metres) from the craft. Then, as Meier looked on amazed, a figure appeared from behind the grounded disc and approached him.

So began the first of more than 100 meetings with cosmonauts from the Pleiades star cluster. In the course of them Meier took some 3000 pages of notes and hundreds of photographs. From his experience came a book: *UFO . . . contact from the Pleiades*. And the whole strange business set off a major controversy among ufologists.

Three 'Pleiadean spacecraft' hover above the Swiss countryside in one of the innumerable sightings claimed by Billy Meier. They have supposedly travelled more than 400 light years to reach the Earth. But they employ a technology so advanced that 'fractions of seconds are sufficient to accomplish light years . . .'

Meier's story was first investigated – and publicised – by Wendelle Stevens, a retired USAF colonel living in Tucson, Arizona. According to Stevens he first heard of the Meier contacts through a niece of the psychologist C. G. Jung, with whom he had been swapping pictures of UFOs for some years. (Stevens is said to have one of the largest collections of UFO photographs in the world.) In 1975 she learned about Meier's pictures, taken only some 35 miles (55 kilometres) from her home, and went to visit Meier. Stevens says that she met eight other witnesses to the Pleiadean contacts during her two-day stay and collected more pictures. Copies of these were sent to Stevens, and in due course the lady arrived in Tucson to see him, bringing some 16 more photographs with her. 'The pictures were super fantastic. I had never seen anything like them before,' said Stevens.

A correspondence then grew up between Stevens and Meier, with Jung's niece acting as courier and translator. 'This went on for eight or nine months before I decided I'd better go and look this guy in the eye. He was taking more and more pictures and they all looked really good.'

Not everyone who looks at Billy Meier's

photographs is as impressed by them, but Stevens duly flew to London and went on to Switzerland by train. There he learned that Meier had begun having unusual and anomalous experiences at the age of five, when he saw a 'large circular craft' fly over the local church. From about that time until the age of eight he heard voices in his head. Then a new voice took over and apparently acted as a guide – 'tutoring' him, according to Stevens. Which was perhaps just as well, for Meier left school at the age of 12 to begin a life of odd-jobbing and oddity, which included car-racing, a short period in jail for thieving, a spell of service with the French Foreign Legion and a couple of years in an Indian ashram – followed by gainful employment in an Indian village as official snake catcher. He worked his way to Turkey, where he claimed to have acted as an informer for US drug-smuggling investigators and so paid his way back to Switzerland.

Exodus in space

While at the ashram, Meier had started to hear voices again. This time they were female and said they were from 'the Dal universe'. While in India he also saw 'spacecraft' once again and took photographs of them – as he also did, apparently, of his female 'Dal' contact. These experiences with the Dals lasted some two years – until, Meier says, their mission to Earth was complete. Then, until 1975, there was silence.

When the Pleiadeans came, there were three of them – Semjase, Ptaah and Asket – and two of them were distinctly female. They had much to tell him. Their home planet is called Erra, and it circles a small sun 'in the system of Taygeta' in the Pleiades cluster. However, this was not their original home: their civilisation had reached great heights on a planet of a star in the constellation of Lyra millions of years previously, but had been unable to cope with its own technological prowess. Before this society finally

Right: Billy Meier had a chequered history even before the Pleiadeans made their alleged contacts with him. It included periods in jail, in the French Foreign Legion and in an Indian ashram. In a former life, he was told, he was a Pleiadean

Above: this is one of the Pleiadean spacecraft types that are capable of interstellar flight, according to Meier. This photograph, lacking ground features or other context, offers few clues to the sceptical analyst trying to judge its authenticity

Left: a Pleiadean spacecraft is just visible beyond Meier's moped in this shot. Time and again he would tour the countryside on the moped in response to strange impulses that were reliable signs of an imminent encounter with the Pleiadeans

tore itself apart in a thermonuclear war, a Lyran named Pleione led a mass exodus into space to colonise planets in the Pleiades, in the Hyades cluster and on a planet of the star Vega. Once the colonists were safely established, space exploration was renewed – bringing the Pleiadeans in due course to our own solar system, which they first reached some thousands of years ago. The cosmonauts told Meier that they reckoned their civilisation was 3000 years in advance of ours on Earth and that 'our sector' of the Universe is governed by the 'Andromeda Council'. The Pleiadeans are also members of a union of planets whose inhabitants number 127 billion people – not superhumans 'but men, like us, benefiting from greater time, and greater knowledge'.

The Pleiades is a group of stars in the constellation of Taurus. To the naked eye it appears to be made up of six or seven stars.

The telescope reveals that these are part of a cluster of many hundreds of stars, 430 light years distant from the Earth. How then, did the cosmonauts ever reach us?

According to them, the journey takes about seven hours and is made in a variety of craft. The barrier posed by the speed of light is broken by a 'hyper-space drive system', and the ships equipped with it are known as 'beamships'. The hyper-space drive apparently works on a 'tachyon system' (tachyons are hypothetical faster-than-light particles). Propulsion below the speed of light is effected by a light-emitting drive. When pressed for more details the cosmonauts told Meier that terrestrial scientists were working on similar systems, known by other names but using the same principles. Five types of craft are used by the Pleiadeans, four of which have an interplanetary capacity – and one of these also has a time-travel mode. The fifth type of craft is used solely for sub-atmospheric reconnaissance.

So, what are the Pleiadeans doing here? And, perhaps a more intriguing question, why was it Billy Meier, a small-time farmer and one-time thief, that they chose to contact?

According to the cosmonauts, their purpose was quite simply to make us aware of the existence of extra-terrestrial life – which was both good and bad by earthly standards, and both human and non-human. Semjase, the elegant lady Pleiadean, put it like this in an early encounter: 'We, too, are still far removed from perfection and have to evolve constantly, just like yourselves. We are neither superior nor superhuman, nor are we missionaries. . . . We feel duty-bound to the citizens of Earth, because our forefathers were your forefathers.' Semjase did not reveal who those common ancestors were, nor was she entirely clear about the nature of the Pleiadean mission:

We have taken on certain tasks, such as, for example, the supervision of developing life in space, particularly human, and to ensure a certain measure of order. In the course of these duties we do here and there approach the denizens of various worlds, select some individuals and instruct them. This we

Below: Semjase, the lovely Pleiadean cosmonaut, had no difficulty, apparently, in communicating with Meier. She and her fellow space travellers were telepathic, and understood his questions before he spoke. Nevertheless, their replies to him were spoken, and were in an oddly accented dialect of Swiss-German

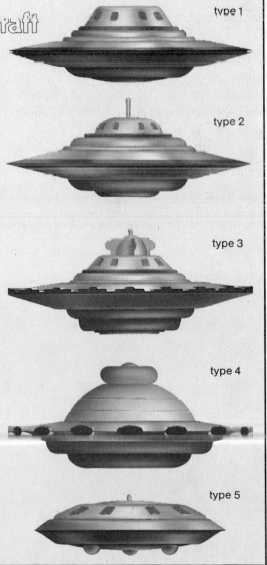

The Pleiadean spacecraft

Billy Meier's photographs show five different types of alleged spacecraft, the functions of which were described to him by Semjase. The first four can travel across interstellar distances by means of a device that transports ship and crew 'in a twinkling of an eye through uncounted light years of distance as we understand it'. A second propulsion system permits travel below the speed of light in the neighbourhood of planets. Artificial gravity can be provided. These craft are 23 feet (7 metres) in diameter, and can be crewed by up to seven cosmonauts, though the usual number is three. Semjase explained that 'our spaceships are protected by a screen of energy which automatically rejects any kind of resistance and every bit of matter. . . .' Interstellar flight calls for transitions through higher dimensions: 'If a spaceship breaks through the barrier of light velocity without reaching hyper-space instantly, a catastrophe is due for ship and crew.'

The fifth type of craft is made in two versions, 12 feet (3.5 metres) and 16 feet (5 metres) in diameter respectively. Used to gather data, they are normally remotely controlled, though the larger models can carry one person. They can be used only in planetary atmospheres.

Pleiadean spacecraft are constantly being developed and improved. Type 1 was superseded after centuries of use because of 'radiation leakage problems'.

type 1

type 2

type 3

type 4

type 5

do only when a race is in a stage of higher evolution. Then we explain (and prove) to them that they are not the only thinking beings in the universe. The Pleiadeans, however, in common with other aliens who have purportedly communicated with people on Earth, are not greatly impressed with the way we are managing our affairs. In the course of their contacts they let it be known to Meier that in their opinion, we terrestrials were not capable of changing mass consciousness, that we were an insane society rushing headlong to our own destruction, that we were not only content with exterminating each other, but we now are bent on destroying all forms of life on this planet as well as the critical life support systems.

Such a state of affairs once pertained when the Pleiadeans inhabited their home system in Lyra, of course: but unlike them, we do not take our world crisis seriously, and no one has made suitable preparations for escape from our doomed planet. Even so, the Pleiadeans refuse to interfere with our way of life or our power structure. We, and we alone, are responsible for our own destiny.

This Zen-like combination of fierce moral comment and studied indifference is driven home by various quasi-mystical utterances by the cosmonauts. Some examples:

Man should know that the God force is quite simply that of creation, and that man also . . . is subject to creation and respectively complementary to it.

Material life on Earth is only a passing event, a phenomenon vanishing after a time. However, before him and after him there continues to exist the creative presence of the universe.

When the spirit, this universal self, manifests itself in the human being through constant love, wisdom and

Above: a fleet of spaceships photographed by Meier in February 1975. He claims to have witnessed them making occasional instantaneous 'jumps' from place to place

Below: a swirl of grass said to have been formed by a spacecraft's landing gear

truth, then a major breakthrough occurs in the surrounding self-veils which eliminates the physical-material urge of greed, anger, hate, avarice, war. . . .

And neither is it consistent with the truth that our brothers and sisters come from other parts of space on behalf of a God to bring to the world the long-awaited peace. In no case do we come on behalf of anybody, since creation, by itself, confers no obligation. It is a law unto itself, and every form of life must conform with it and become a part of it.

Thus spoke Semjase, Pleiadean cosmonaut, to Billy Meier during 1975.

But why was it Meier that was chosen? Wendelle Stevens believes he knows the answer: 'They told him that they had been in contact with him before in other lifetimes.' Such an idea might, of course, occur to someone who had spent two years listening to the kind of conversation that takes place daily in an ashram. But Meier's belief is a little more elaborate, according to Stevens's testimony:

They said that their ancestors had contacted him during prior incarnations on Earth. They told him that he was one of them who had been caught in an Earth evolution by his own choice several thousand years ago. Since his soul patterns were more akin to them it was registered in their computers. Supposedly, they could find him wherever he was. As he was one of them and familiar with their mission, his soul could understand ideas communicated to him better than our souls could. The Pleiadean computer, it will be noted, is obviously a remarkable piece of machinery, able to record 'soul patterns'. But then, it is not clear how material the cosmonauts are themselves. The delectable Semjase told Meier that when coming to Earth the Pleiadeans 'are forced into making a "slight adjustment" which allows us to function properly within your dimensional world'. Without such an 'adjustment', no extra-terrestrial could make contact with people on Earth. It ensures 'a correct state of mind and corresponds with the human vibrational pattern'.

This may (or may not) have something to do with the high level of spiritual development claimed by the Pleiadeans. Using their telepathic powers, they are apparently able to think in concert, 'exercising their astute powers of purity of thought' to control their tendencies to discord and strife. Thus freed from bickering, their technology has flourished and so has their medicine, giving the Pleiadeans an average life expectancy of 1000 years.

Despite these talents, Meier observed, the cosmonauts spoke in an oddly accented form of Swiss-German. The remarkable nature of the Pleiadean computer is seemingly responsible, as Semjase explained:

We are in possession of all Earth languages which are spoken at the moment or have ever been spoken in past ages. We have exact data on them from which we have developed language courses. This happens through computer-like apparatus under the supervision of language experts. . . . Other types of apparatus may serve to connect us to the 'computer' in such a way to make it virtually possible for the languages to be inspired into us. . . .

Such a process, it seems, is still unable to induce a perfect accent.

And the question is still unresolved as to quite what the Pleiadeans expected Meier to *do* with all this information – unless they foresaw his contact with Colonel Stevens and the resulting publicity. Once familiar with the outlines of the case, Stevens certainly lost no time in gathering the evidence: photographs, metal samples given Meier by the cosmonauts, physical traces of the landings, film, tape recordings, computer analysis of pictures, statements from other witnesses, all gathered in a total of 62 days spent with Meier in Switzerland. But what is the significance of that investigation?

UFOs in the sunset. Two photographs taken within a short time of each other, showing 'spacecraft' of two different types manoeuvring over Meier's farm, visible in the background (below left). To seasoned ufologists, pictures as spectacular as this seem 'too good to be true', but Colonel Wendelle Stevens rapidly became convinced of their authenticity and has staunchly defended them

Billy Meier's tales of meetings with space people are not marked by restraint. This chapter recounts more of these amazing claims — and describes the intellectual contortions of Meier's supporters

SWISS FARMER BILLY MEIER'S claim to have had over 130 meetings with cosmonauts from the Pleiades star cluster between 1975 and 1978 is perhaps the most elaborately documented contactee case in the literature of ufology. For Meier supported his story not only with a mass of photographs but with samples of metal allegedly given him by the Pleiadeans, with tape recordings of their craft in flight, and, according to Colonel Wendelle Stevens (who first investigated the affair), produced other witnesses to the remarkable events that he described. All this evidence was, Stevens says, subjected to rigorous scientific testing – and was passed as authentic. The results of Stevens's investigation were published in the United States in 1979 in a lavish book called *UFO . . . contact from the Pleiades.*

Material that has surfaced since then, together with further revelations by the seemingly irrepressible Billy Meier, may

Right: a Pleiadean craft, enabled to make its rendezvous with Meier by detecting his 'brain wave patterns'. According to the Pleiadeans, this process 'normally enables our computer/auto-pilot to direct our beam ship to the exact location without interference'

Below: one of the outmoded Variation Type-1 spacecraft

A mass of contradictions

lead one to wonder just what Meier's purpose is in all this. For his story has now become so bizarre that even the most gullible devotee of the extra-terrestrial hypothesis ought to be feeling just the teeniest twinges of doubt. And that is without knowing the results of the independent scientific tests of the evidence that have been carried out.

The most startling of Meier's later claims is to have been taken in one of the Pleiadean spacecraft (known as Variation Type-4, apparently) on a journey through time. On this trip, says Meier, he went back to the age of the dinosaurs and photographed them; he also visited Jesus Christ, who was so impressed with Meier that he appointed him a disciple. Meier says he returned to this day and age in order to avoid being crucified. He also claims to have visited other planets, to have photographed the link-up between the Apollo and Soyuz spacecraft as he flew by

(odd that neither NASA nor the Russians seemed aware of the Pleiadeans flitting past), and, most extravagant of all, to have taken a photograph of the eye of God. Meier also was taken into the future by the Pleiadeans to see San Francisco come to a sticky end, sinking into the bay as the San Andreas fault at last produced its much-heralded catastrophe.

These tales have naturally attracted some laughter, and Meier's responses to his critics have scarcely helped his case. When asked why he failed to photograph both eyes of God, for example, he replied that the other was closed: the Lord was winking at his companion (who was, needless to say, the shapely Pleiadean Semjase). Other 'evidence' is so peculiar as to need no comment – such as the photograph of a pterodactyl that shows a pyramid in the background!

As Meier's defenders – mainly the group known as Genesis III, who published Colonel Stevens's book on the Meier case – have attempted to come to the rescue, they too have fallen into confusion and contradiction. Or perhaps worse. The chief critic of the Meier case has been Kal Korff, and the title of his book on the subject sums up his attitude more than adequately: *The most infamous hoax in ufology.*

One instance of self-contradiction on the part of Meier and his defenders concerns a sequence of photographs purporting to show a Pleiadean spacecraft circling a tree. An

unfortunate aspect of this series is that when independent investigators visited the site, no tree was to be found. Meier's explanation for this was that the spacecraft had subsequently disintegrated the hapless arboreal specimen. When taxed with the same question, Wendelle Stevens told Korff that the tree vanished because it had been teleported into 'another time frame'. Kal Korff's suspicion is that neither of these things happened, since a close look at the pictures – reputedly taken within a few seconds of one another – reveals markedly different cloud patterns from frame to frame. Genesis III's claim that the day in question was particularly windy is not borne out by the weather record, which shows wind speeds reaching a maximum of 15 miles per hour (25 km/h). Korff reasons that a model UFO and model tree were superimposed on pictures of the site. And indeed models of the Pleiadean craft have been found on the Meier farm – though Meier says that they were inspired by his actual encounters.

Possibly the least plausible of Meier's

Above: a spacecraft circles a tree in this sequence shot by Meier. In other frames, the tree's top is alleged to move, owing to the 'force' of the craft. But according to hostile photographic analysts, the pictures are the result of superimposing the UFO and tree images onto the background sequence. The cloud patterns could not have changed so much, they say, in the short time that the UFO was allegedly circling the tree

defenders is Jim Dilettoso, of Genesis III. Kal Korff prints a long interview with him (and dismantles most of his statements) in which he says that in the 1950s Wendelle Stevens and another ufologist, Richard Miller, performed something called 'transchannelling' on aliens for the US Air Force:

They would fly up to Alaska because they were told that the magnetic fields there were proper for resonance induction, and we have hundreds and hundreds of audio recordings of Richard and other CIA officers doing transchannelings of aliens. . . . Two of those CIA officers . . . have developed serious personality aberrations.

Asked why, Dilettoso replied:

. . . it seems like something consistent in people that do channeling . . . that their cell-salt structures change, and they develop diabetes.

There's also studies done that the last two Popes developed diabetes, as do a lot of Eastern gurus. So what's the correlation between transchanneling and cell-salts and diabetes, then diabetes going unchecked, developing into other neurotic and schizophrenic . . . behaviors that usually show up as olfactory and motor sense disturbances like Parkinson's disease. It's not where they become schizophrenic where their thinking is impaired, but where their body reactions are affected, and Billy [Meier] shows signs of that also. . . .

But that seems consistent in the, oh . . . some thousand contactee cases that are being studied. In that the vibrating field put out by the ship and by the beings themselves *dominates* the aura, the magnetic field that can be kirlian photographed, dominates it so much, that it appears to even get down and start reprogramming the DNA.

One may be forgiven for suspecting that Stevens, and his associates who make up Genesis III, did start by believing Meier and accepting his evidence at face value. Then, embarrassed by the jeers, laughter and protests of more painstaking ufologists, they were forced into defending their lost cause. Meier, however, has simply continued to make ever more extravagant comments – not, perhaps, without a certain impish humour – which Genesis III have tumbled over themselves to make respectable. The results, after the fashion of tumbling, bear a close resemblance to slapstick, however. The paucity of photographs of the Pleiadeans themselves is explained by Wendelle Stevens

A spacecraft hovers in the distant sky beyond the tripod-mounted camera. The telepathic promptings that Meier received before each encounter enabled him to come to it well-prepared with such photographic equipment as he possessed – which, however, was somewhat inadequate to the world-shaking nature of these events

thus: 'They are afraid of being hurt . . . they do not want to be recognised. Supposedly, they do walk the streets in Europe and don't wish to be compromised.' Billy Meier, on the other hand, has happily admitted the strong resemblance between Semjase and his own girlfriend – so who is really worried about being recognised on the streets of Europe?

Less edifying are the claims made by Meier and Genesis III concerning the samples of metal and crystal given Meier by the Pleiadeans as examples of their technological wizardry. Meier actually produced these while Stevens and his team were in Switzerland. They called on him one morning and were told that he had had his 105th contact during the night and 'had a surprise' for the investigators. This turned out to be a package, handed over by the cosmonaut Quetzal, of four metal, one biological and nine mineral and crystal specimens. According to the book, the scientists who conducted 'in-depth, highly sophisticated examination' of these samples found them to have unique qualities and said they had 'never seen anything like it before'. The level of purity in the metal was 'not immediately explainable' while the general characteristics 'seemed to indicate a non-electrolytic, cold fusion synthesis process not generally known to earth technology'.

Kal Korff found rather less to be excited about. He interviewed Dr Marcel Vogel, who had analysed the samples for Genesis III – and had drawn rather different conclusions

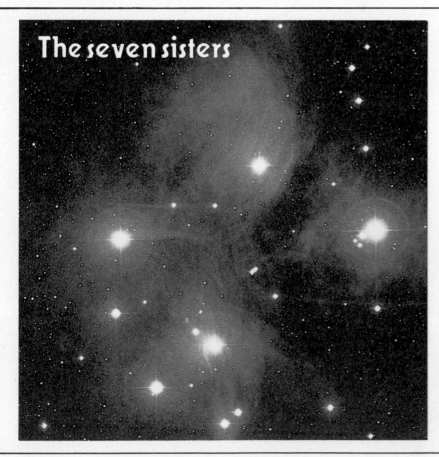

The seven sisters

The Pleiades (left), the star cluster that is the home of the space people with whom Billy Meier claims to meet so regularly. The haze of gas and dust indicates the comparative youth of the cluster, for as the group matures the interstellar matter will disperse. The few hundred stars of the cluster were born together a mere 60 million years ago – by contrast with the 5000 million years of the Sun's existence to date. This time is too short to have permitted the formation of any planets, or the appearance of indigenous life. According to Meier, the space people migrated to the Pleiades from their original home in the constellation of Lyra. But how do they survive there? Is Erra, their supposed home, an artificial planet constructed by the migrants?

The Pleiades of Greek myth were seven sisters, named Alcyone, Asterope, Electra, Celaeno, Maia, Merope and Taygeta. They were daughters of Atlas and Pleione. As it happens, the leader of the migration from Lyra was called Pleione, according to Meier. Was the mythical name a faint memory of the space traveller? Or was the space traveller's name suggested to Meier by the half-remembered mythical name?

from those published in the book. Only the first sample was unique, said Dr Vogel, consisting of aluminium, silver and thulium, each having a high degree of purity. The other samples were ordinary crystals of quartz, citrine, amethyst and silver solder, and there is no reason to believe they are of extra-terrestrial origin. Jim Dilettoso characteristically failed to further the cause by claiming that Genesis III hold a 10-hour videotape of 'the entire lab proceedings' (which Dr Vogel denies having made). 'And,' Dilettoso incautiously persisted, 'we have about an hour of him discussing why the metal samples are not possible in earth technology, going into intrinsic detail of why it is not done anywhere on earth, that type of chemistry.' Of course, Dr Vogel may not be the only scientist to have analysed the samples (no mention is made by either party of the biological specimen), but then Genesis III are notably coy about naming any of the 200 scientists they say have verified Meier's remarkable story.

They are no less reticent about the numerous other witnesses who, they say, saw – and in some cases photographed – the Pleiadean craft skimming around the Swiss valleys. No other photographs have surfaced, none are printed in the book, and none of these other witnesses are named. The best the book offers is a number of photographs of unidentified people sitting around Billy Meier's dining table and the assertion that tapes of conversations with the witnesses were subjected to psychological stress evaluation (PSE). The pictures by themselves prove absolutely nothing, while PSE is a notoriously unreliable method of lie detection, despite Genesis III's talk of 'special computers standing by in northern California' to perform the analysis.

Genesis III do not mention any analysis of the notes made by Meier of his contacts

Above: witnesses pose for Meier's camera – seemingly too blasé about spacecraft to heed the hovering disc

Below: the fortunate Meier merits visits by whole squadrons of spacecraft

with the Pleiadeans. But Jim Lorenzen of APRO quotes Dr James Hurtak, a language specialist who has taken the opportunity to read most of the 3000 pages of the 'Semjase correspondence' in the original German. 'The linguistic use of Egyptian-Aramaic and Egyptian-Hebrew names . . . is "latterday patchwork",' he says. 'All this shifting play of correspondences by which everything . . . is cheated of its individual logic creates a mood of pensive jesting . . . and even sublime travesty. By all the standards of genuine "ancient knowledge" . . . this civilisation which lays claim to being 3000 years into the future has not offered much in the way of a quantum jump over what our ancestors had 5000 years ago (in the way of intellectual transformation).'

'The aliens gave Meier the most sought after prize of all – wisdom,' remarks Kal Korff, adding: 'It was very basic wisdom indeed.' Certainly, reading through the pronouncements on life, the Universe and everything that Semjase condescended to give Meier (see page 43), one is embarrassed by their half-familiar triviality.

But of all the evidence produced by Meier, none is as controversial as his photographs of Pleiadean spacecraft.

The camera never lies?

Massive scientific expertise has vindicated Billy Meier's spacecraft photographs, according to his supporters. These claims however should be pitted against the rather different conclusions of skilled ufologists

THE PHOTOGRAPHS TAKEN by 'Billy' Meier of Pleiadean spacecraft as they flew around the valleys near Hinwel, Switzerland, are among the most striking UFO pictures ever published. They are so striking that they evoke that paradoxical response: *too* good to be true. But after a while one realises, looking at these elegant productions, that one's instinct has backed away from them for a less cynical reason: the pictures simply don't *fit* with one's sense of light and shade as seen in the real world. They are visually disjointed, offending one's sense of balance, clashing with one's memory of how things look. Then, on a closer look, certain patterns in the pictures emerge – and certain suspicions are aroused.

Is it coincidence, for example, that so many pictures of the same craft seem to show the flying disc at exactly the same angle to the camera, despite the very different locations and times of day at which the pictures were supposedly taken? Why do the reflections and shadows on the Pleiadean spaceships appear the same, too, despite the various backgrounds? Why are the undersides of the craft always so dark – as they would be if they

A Type-4 spacecraft over Mount Auruti, Switzerland, photographed by Billy Meier on 29 March 1976 (above). Two computer-enhanced images made from this photograph (above right) reveal a great deal about this picture. The left-hand image shows, in the words of Ground Saucer Watch who made the computer analyses, 'evidence of a linear structure' above the craft – in plain English, a string or a thin rod supporting the object. The structure is equally clear in tho computerised enlargement in the second image. In addition, study of the focus in this picture indicates that the object is close to the camera and is therefore small – about 8 inches (20 centimetres) across, not 23 feet (7 metres) as claimed

were models, say, close to the camera? Why does only one picture, of extremely low quality, exist of a landed disc? Is there any significance in the massive preponderance of shots in which the craft are shown against a clear, light sky – the best type of background on which to superimpose a UFO image?

Wendelle Stevens and Genesis III – whom it seems fair to call both investigators and publicists of the Meier case – have their own answers to some of these questions. In an interview with the ufologist Timothy Green Beckley, Wendelle Stevens rather disarmingly remarked:

First of all, photographs are poor evidence because there are so many things that we can do technically to produce images. However, there are also so many ways we can detect a hoax. We can tell if we are dealing with superimposed overlays, reflected images, double exposures. We can tell by looking through special microscopes and searching for grain density and grain patterns. We can pretty much tell if an object has been thrown into the air or suspended by something in the air.

And in keeping with that scepticism, the book published by Genesis III, *UFO . . . contact from the Pleiades*, shows computer-processed versions of the photographs that appear to validate their authenticity. It is when Wendelle Stevens starts to explain some of the computer enhancements that the reader's credulity is stretched. Says the colonel:

We can [analyse photographs] with a computer by studying the edges around any given object. In high magnification an edge is seen as a series of shock waves. There is a special formula for the spacing of these shock waves that make up the edge. How strong they are, how far apart they are, will tell you how far apart that edge of the object is from the camera. If the body is in

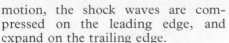

motion, the shock waves are compressed on the leading edge, and expand on the trailing edge.

In fact, nothing of the kind happens. What this particular computer process does is enhance the picture contrast in areas where the image brightness varies – especially at the edges of features, making it possible to make judgements about how far the object photographed is from the camera. In some cases, it is possible to intensify otherwise hard-to-detect strings or supports attached to the object. This has nothing whatever to do with shock waves, though Stevens has repeated the idea more than once.

In Genesis III's book, the 12 or so pictures purporting to show analytic enhancements of Meier's pictures are accompanied by details of the various tests to which the photographs were subjected. It is claimed that the computer enhancements showed how the light

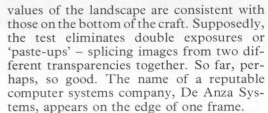

William H. Spaulding, Director of the Western Division of Ground Saucer Watch (GSW), at the console of the image-processing computer with which GSW analyse UFO photographs. GSW's verdict on the Meier pictures that they studied: 'total hoaxes'

values of the landscape are consistent with those on the bottom of the craft. Supposedly, the test eliminates double exposures or 'paste-ups' – splicing images from two different transparencies together. So far, perhaps, so good. The name of a reputable computer systems company, De Anza Systems, appears on the edge of one frame.

Kal Korff took the simple step of asking Mr Wayne Heppler, manager of De Anza Systems, if an analysis had been performed for Genesis III. Replied the honest Mr Heppler:

What these guys did was come down to De Anza Systems claiming that they wanted to *buy* a computer from us. So we took one of their pictures, one showing the UFO, and enhanced it to make certain parts of the picture stand out. Then they took pictures of it, left, and stated they would get back in touch with us. And we haven't heard from them since.

Korff then asked if De Anza had the technical capability to analyse the pictures. The

answer: 'No. We are in no position to do an analysis.'

At a lecture at the UFO '80 Symposium held in Oakland, California, in August 1980, Jim Dilettoso of Genesis III said that 'z-scale contouring' and 'edge identification' tests were run on the pictures. The only drawback to this is that these are simply colour contouring techniques (and can be used to analyse the 'density' at each point of an image – its lightness or darkness). They are *not* light distortion tests, such as edge enhancement, which might reveal the information Genesis III claim to have gained by the techniques.

Dilettoso also (perhaps rather rashly) took exception to a Ground Saucer Watch (GSW) colour contouring of one of the Meier pictures. This shows a similar level of light reflectivity on both the ground and the Pleiadean spacecraft – indicating that *something* is wrong with the photograph, since the

This photograph (left) was taken within a few minutes of the one on the previous page. The craft is said to be hovering beyond the tree, which is about 165 feet (50 metres) away. Two computer-processed versions appear opposite. The edge enhancement on the left revealed, according to GSW, inconsistencies between the shadows on the disc and on the tree. This suggests that the UFO and landscape images have been superimposed. The colour-contoured image on the right suggested to GSW that the UFO image was actually superimposed *on top* of the tree image, as if the UFO were closer than the tree – 'indicating very sloppy work', in Kal Korff's words

materials, at the claimed distances, should reflect (and so colour contour) differently. Dilettoso's objection was unfortunate, since even Genesis III's computer-generated picture shows both the craft and its background in the same colour contour.

It did so, Kal Korff discovered, for reasons that could prove nothing about the authenticity of Billy Meier's photographs. According to Ken Dimwiddie, one of the technicians at De Anza Systems, who was present when Dilettoso appeared in the guise of a prospective customer, it was Dilettoso himself who assigned the colours on the computer's read-out screen. In other words, the colours may indicate almost anything about the actual qualities of the original photograph. They have little value except to satisfy Jim Dilettoso's aesthetic fancy.

Computer-aided analyses of the Meier

Below: this picture, from a scorched negative found in Meier's barn, was never intended by him to be published. It shows, unmistakably, a model spacecraft on a table-top. Meier admitted that he possessed models of the Pleiadean craft – made by his children from his descriptions, he insisted

Below right: Billy Meier kneels between Wendelle Stevens (writing) and Lee Elders, co-author of *UFO . . . contact from the Pleiades*. The child is Meier's youngest son

pictures by Ground Saucer Watch, however, are devastating by comparison. They inspired two GSW researchers, Fred Adrian and William Spaulding, to describe them as 'hoaxes, both crude and grandiose'.

Even without the aid of computer enhancement the photographs are dubious. Shadows on the Pleiadean craft do not conform to the light in the landscape, and the sharpness of the UFO images indicates that the object shown is extremely close to the camera – as a model would be. (GSW's estimate is that the various 'spaceships' are, in fact, between 8 and 12 inches [20 and 30 centimetres] in diameter.) Fuzziness that would result from atmospheric effects is often lacking.

Where the images are more consistent with expectations, one is still left baffled by the testimony of Meier himself. Despite his

constant contacts and the priceless photographic evidence he was gathering on behalf of mankind, Meier never bothered to repair or replace his allegedly broken camera, whose lens was stuck, focused at infinity. Yet different focusings *do* seem to have been achieved – resulting in 'distant' objects coming out as suitably fuzzy.

But then the testimony concerning Meier and his photographic techniques occasionally leaves the disinterested enquirer gasping. It should be pointed out that Billy Meier lost his left arm in an accident, which one would expect to make for difficulties with a camera. Wendelle Stevens nevertheless has made the startling claim that Meier shot all his pictures from the hip, because the mirror in his camera had 'jammed closed' as well. And yet he manages to centre his UFOs in every frame with amazing precision.

Jim Dilettoso also says that a professional photographic expert claimed he would need 'a million dollars' to duplicate the Meier pictures. Less excitably, Wendelle Stevens attempts to debunk the claims that the UFOs are models by asking: 'How many models can a one-armed man carry on a moped when he is driving with the only arm he's got?' One might reply: 'As many as will fit in a bag.'

So, what is one to make of the Meier case?

Certainly, the material evidence is anything but convincing, and the tales told by Meier have (as GSW have pointed out) all the hallmarks of American George Adamski's extravaganzas, updated and technically sophisticated for a more demanding age.

It is disheartening to learn that Stevens received an invitation to present his case to the House of Lords UFO Committee, who should have known better than to invite him in the first place.

Genesis III come out of the affair in greater embarrassment than Meier, who, after all, is apparently renowned for being 'a sort of person who gets great satisfaction out of fooling the authorities'. Genesis III have published some remarkable claims on behalf of Meier, yet none of those claims has been validated by independent research. Wendelle Stevens may attempt to disarm

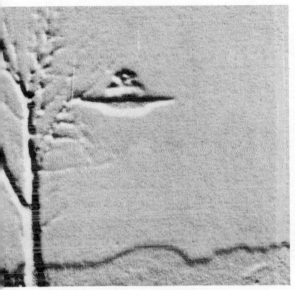

Left: Meier reported that these discs were photographed about 1½ hours after the one seen above and on the previous pages. GSW found that the focus on the discs is much sharper than on the trees, showing that the discs are much closer. Again, there is evidence that the UFO images were superimposed on the landscape picture

the ufologist Jim Lorenzen by saying, 'As you well know, Jim, the book was never designed to present any hard facts,' yet it gives every impression of doing just that.

As for Meier himself, it is possible that some *subjective* experience lies behind the discredited material evidence. If the stories of voices in the head, going for rides in 'pear-shaped UFOs' with 'a very old man' at the age of five, and the sightings he had from a very early age are anything to go by, this may be the best explanation. In which case, the model spacecraft (whose existence Meier doesn't deny) may well have been constructed as a result of an actual series of contactee experiences, however unlikely it is that these represent an attempt by any Pleiadeans to get in touch with us on Earth. If so, then Billy Meier has unfortunately allowed his experience to be turned by others into something like an industry.

The British scareship invasion

A policeman's sighting of a huge and mysterious airship early in 1909 started a spate of reports of similar terrifying craft. Were they, asks NIGEL WATSON, German Zeppelins – or were they something much stranger?

IN THE EARLY MONTHS of 1909 an aerial horror began to haunt the imaginations of the British people. The first sighting of a phantom airship to have a major impact on the public consciousness was made by a Cambridgeshire policeman, PC Kettle. He was patrolling Cromwell Road in Peterborough on the morning of 23 March when he heard the sound of a distant motor car. As he continued to 'hear the steady buzz of a high power engine' he suddenly realised that the noise was coming from above. On looking up he saw a bright light attached to a long oblong body outlined against the stars. This strange aerial object crossed the sky at a high speed, and was soon lost from sight.

News of this sighting was met with a certain amount of scepticism. Nevertheless, it set the pattern for future 'airship' watchers: reports from people who had seen bright, powerful lamps or searchlights attached to dark bodies making a noisy passage across the night sky soon became numerous. Another common feature of such stories was the happy habit of many self-proclaimed experts of submitting explanations for such marvellous visions. In the case of PC Kettle's sighting, a Peterborough police officer announced to the press that a 'very fine kite flying over the neighbourhood of Cobden

Above: an early dirigible, the Zeppelin Mark 2, in flight over Lake Constance in April 1909. The same year, there was a spate of mystery airship sightings throughout Britain. Many people believed that the aircraft were German Zeppelins making reconnaissance flights in preparation for an invasion of Britain – but German airships were far too unreliable for it to be possible to employ them on such a dangerous mission

Below: Cromwell Road, Peterborough, the site of the first 'scareship' sighting

Street' had been the cause. The bright light was easily explained as a Chinese lantern that had been attached to the kite.

'But how about the matter of the airship going at a tremendous pace?' asked a reporter.

'Oh, that was a little poetic touch on Kettle's part for the benefit of you interviewers. He did not officially report that, and the wind driving the kite would give the impression of movement,' replied the officer.

'But how do you get over the whirring and beating of engines?' asked the still puzzled reporter.

'Oh, that,' responded the officer, as he went to take his leave, 'was the motor which goes all night in the Co-operative Bakery in Cobden Street!'

This bland dismissal of PC Kettle's observation might have carried more weight if it had been released soon after the sighting.

Instead, it took the Peterborough police at least six weeks to arrive at this simple answer to the mystery of the airship. It seems they preferred to imply that PC Kettle was a simpleton who could not distinguish between a kite and an airship, rather than to see the Peterborough police force implicated in giving credence to such an unlikely story.

At first PC Kettle's observation seemed an isolated occurrence. But around the beginning of May sightings began to be reported daily throughout south-east England. A typical report was made by a Mr C. W. Allen. As he and some friends were driving through

Right: a clipping from the Cardiff *Evening Express and Evening Mail* of Wednesday, 19 May 1909 describes a sighting of the mystery airship made by Mr C. Lethbridge on 18 May on Caerphilly Mountain. Mr Lethbridge saw a huge 'long, tube-shaped object' lying on the grass at the side of the road. Newspaper cuttings relating to airship sightings and to German military matters were later found scattered over the area

the village of Kelmarsh, Northamptonshire, on 13 May, they heard a loud bang. Then above them they heard the 'tock-tock-tock' sound of a motor engine. Although the sky was dark they were able to see a 100-foot (30-metre) long torpedo-shaped airship that carried lights fore and aft. It was moving swiftly, but this did not prevent the witnesses seeing a platform suspended beneath the craft, which appeared to contain its crew. The airship disappeared in the direction of Peterborough.

There were many more such reports. But what were the aircraft? The fact that the exploits of Count Zeppelin were well-known in Britain (see box), combined with the antagonism between Germany and Britain, soon led people to believe that German airships were making a reconnaissance in preparation for a future invasion.

Below: the Wellman airship at the Aero Show of 1909. Prior to the First World War, Britain devoted very little research to airships; government construction was begun in 1907, but at the outbreak of war in 1914 only five British ships had been built

The major flaw in the hypothesis, however, was the sheer number of airship sighting reports, which came from all regions of Britain. At the time, Germany barely had the resources to make even one or two reconnaissance flights over Britain. For this reason, a few newspapers were prepared to discount the entire phenomenon as imaginary, and sent readers who had reported airship sightings to what they picturesquely called 'lunacy experts'. From one expert, they received this diagnosis:

> In every thousand men there are always two every night who see strange matters – chromatic rats, luminous owls, moving lights, fiery comets, and things like those. So you can always get plenty of evidence of this sort, particularly when you suggest it to the patient first.

The most puzzling and sensational sighting was made by an elderly Punch and Judy showman, Mr C. Lethbridge. With this report, made on 18 May, the focus for the airship's activities shifted from the east coast to mid Glamorgan, Wales. By now there were well-attested reports of a 'long-shaped

A phantom fleet?

Could the mysterious airships seen over Britain during 1909 have been German Zeppelins? It seems unlikely.

The pioneer of German airship research was Count Ferdinand von Zeppelin (right), who launched his first dirigible, the *Luftschiff Zeppelin 1* – or *LZ1* – over Lake Constance in July 1900, shortly before his sixty-second birthday. *LZ1*, simply an enormous bag filled with gas and propelled by an engine, remained in the air for just over 17 minutes – but its short flight was impressive, and

the future of airships seemed bright.

Count Zeppelin set in motion an ambitious airship-building programme, but by 1909, owing to a number of crashes and shortage of money, there were only three working Zeppelins in existence – the *LZ3*, rebuilt from an earlier airship that had crashed, the *LZ5* and the *LZ6*. Of these, only two, the *LZ3* and the *LZ5*, were in the hands of the army – and they were very much in their experimental stages, and certainly not capable of long and hazardous journeys, or of carrying out the high-speed manoeuvres reported by the witnesses of the British 'scareships'.

object' with red flashing lights seen over Belfast, Ireland, on 17 May, and there seemed to be no area of Britain left unaffected by the scare. A few hours after his sighting – which amounted to a close encounter – Mr Lethbridge told inquisitive reporters:

Yesterday I went to Senghenydd and proceeded to walk home over Caerphilly Mountain. You know that the top of the mountain is a very lonely spot. I reached it about 11 p.m., and when turning the bend at the summit I was surprised to see a long, tube-shaped affair lying on the grass at the roadside, with two men busily engaged with something nearby. They attracted my close attention because of their peculiar get-up; they appeared to have

big, heavy fur coats and fur caps fitting tightly over their heads. I was rather frightened, but I continued to go on until I was within twenty yards [18 metres] of them and then my idea as to their clothing was confirmed. The noise of my little spring-cart seemed to attract them and when they saw me they jumped up and jabbered furiously to each other in a strange lingo – Welsh or something else; it was certainly not English. They hurriedly collected something from the ground, and then I was really frightened. The long thing on the ground rose up slowly. I was standing still all the time, quite amazed, and when it was hanging a few feet off the ground the men jumped into

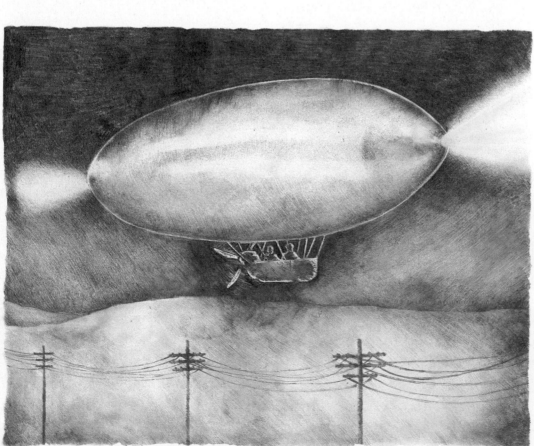

Left: the 'scareship' seen by Mr C. Lethbridge on Caerphilly Mountain on 18 May 1909 'rose in the air in a zig-zag fashion' and sailed away towards Cardiff

Right: Ham Common, on the outskirts of London. Here, on the night of 13 May 1909, a Mr Grahame and a Mr Bond saw a remarkable airship whose pilots, whom they described as a Yankee and a German, apparently steered their craft by pulling beer handles

Right: the village of Kelmarsh, Northamptonshire where, on 13 May 1909, a Mr C. W. Allen saw a 100-foot (30-metre) airship moving swiftly north-eastwards

Below: a cartoon published in *Punch* of 26 May 1909. The cartoon shows a sea serpent staring glumly at a headline in the *Daily Scare*: 'Mysterious air-ship seen everywhere by night' – and commenting, 'Well, if this sort of thing keeps on, it'll mean a dull August for me'

a kind of little carriage suspended from it, and gradually the whole affair and the men rose in the air in a zig-zag fashion. When they had cleared the telegraph wires that pass over the mountain, two lights like electric lamps shone out, and the thing went higher into the air and sailed away towards Cardiff.

When Mr Lethbridge, accompanied by reporters, returned to the site where he had his encounter, they found several traces of the airship's presence. The ground where the 45-foot (14-metre) long object had been seen was churned up as though by a plough-share. All over the area they discovered a quantity of newspaper cuttings of accounts of airship sightings and references to the German emperor and army. Along with these items they found a large quantity of papier-mâché packing material, a lid from a tin of metal polish, a few dozen pieces of blue paper bearing strange writing, and a metal pin with a red label attached to it. The label of the pin carried instructions in French and excited attention when some commentators thought that it was part of an explosive device, but further enquiry showed it probably to have been a valve plunger for a motor car tyre.

Several witnesses came forward to support Lethbridge's story. In Salisbury Road, Cathays, Cardiff, residents said that on the same evening, between 10.40 and 10.50 p.m., they saw an airship-like object in the air.

Cigar-shaped 'boat'
Additional testimony came from workers on Cardiff docks who, two hours after Lethbridge's encounter, saw a fast moving 'boat of cigar shape' flying from the direction of Newport, and going eastwards. The airship carried two lights, and its engines made a loud whirring noise. One witness said, 'We could not see those on board. The airship was too high up for that at night, but it was plain that it was a big airship.'

Two gentlemen, a Mr Grahame and a Mr Bond, made some even more extravagant claims, to the effect that they had seen a 200- to 230-foot (60- to 70-metre) long airship 'like a collection of big cigar boxes with the ends out' on Ham Common, London. The occupants of the craft, whom they met on the night of 13 May, they described as a clean-shaven Yankee and a German who smoked a calabash pipe. The German asked for some tobacco, which Mr Grahame supplied out of his own pouch. Although they were blinded by a searchlight that played on their faces, the witnesses were able to see that the 'Yankee' was positioned in a kind of wire cage, and in front of him he had a row of levers similar to draught beer pump handles. In front of the German was positioned a map with pins dotted all over it. The encounter apparently came to an abrupt end when the 'Yankee' pulled one of the levers down, 'and then he switched the light off, and the aeroplane went without either of the men saying good-bye.'

With such a variety of bizarre reports, it is hardly surprising that the mystery of the phantom scareship that plagued Britain in 1909 has proved difficult to solve.

Who sent the scareships?

When the 1909 epidemic of 'scareship' sightings died down, it seemed to be the end of the story – until, in 1912, new and more mysterious sightings began to be reported

RUMOURS OF A FLIGHT by a Zeppelin airship over Sheerness, Kent, on the evening of 14 October 1912 caused questions to be asked in the House of Commons. On 27 November 1912, opposition MP Mr William Joynson-Hicks asked the First Lord of the Admiralty, Mr Winston Churchill, if he knew anything about this matter. Mr Churchill affirmed that an unidentified aircraft had been reported on that date. It was heard flying over the district at 7 p.m., and caused flares to be lit at nearby Eastchurch in anticipation of a landing by the craft. However, nothing descended from the night sky, and the nationality and origin of the craft, Mr Churchill had to admit, remained a mystery.

Enquiries by the press in Eastchurch revealed that the townspeople had heard a buzzing noise between 6.30 and 7 p.m. on 14 October. But at the time it was assumed to be the sound of an airship or aeroplane making its way to the naval aviation school at Eastchurch. This was not the case, however, for no aircraft made any night flight on the date in question, from or to that base.

The public discussion that followed in the wake of the exchange between Mr Joynson-Hicks and Mr Churchill had many unforeseen consequences.

Almost immediately the German *L1* Zeppelin, which had started a 30-hour proving flight on 13 October, was blamed as the cause of the Sheerness incident. Whether or not the *L1*, or any other of Germany's airships, visited Sheerness in 1912 is still a matter for debate. Whatever the reason for the incident, the British government decided to strengthen the Aerial Navigation Act of 1911, in order to pacify public and official disquiet. The bill was quickly passed through parliamentary channels and was given the royal assent on 14 February 1913. It gave the Home Secretary the power to prohibit aerial traffic over areas of the United Kingdom and its territorial waters. It also meant that if an aerial vehicle failed to respond to ground signals, or violated the prohibited areas, it was liable to be fired at.

Not everybody was pleased with the amended act. Feverish efforts were made to construct an efficient sky gun – but while the project remained in its experimental stages,

The state of the art

The government of the day claimed it knew nothing of the 'scareships' of 1913. Could this really have been the case? The first two army airships, the *Nulli Secundus* I and II, had been dismantled by 1909; the first of the smaller airships that followed them, the *Beta*, made its maiden flight in 1910. Clearly whatever caused the 1909 sightings could not have been an army machine. The same applies to the 1913 sightings. The successors of the *Beta* – the *Gamma* and *Delta* – were too small to be mistaken for 'scareships', and two airships ordered from France, and one made in Britain by Vickers, had met with disaster.

There remains the possibility that some of the Welsh sightings may be explained as misidentifications of airships built by the only private manufacturer of note, E.T. Willows of Cardiff. But these ships were familiar to local people; Captain Lindsay, for example, actually compared the 'scareship' he saw over Cardiff on 17 January 1913 with the Willows airship. The mystery remains.

Left: the Krupp 6.5-centimetre gun, designed in Germany in 1909 for shooting down airships, shown with an artist's impression of a Zeppelin. Sightings of an unidentified airship over Kent in October 1912 led opposition MP Mr William Joynson-Hicks (inset) to ask questions in the House of Commons; and in 1913 parliament passed a bill that meant that any unauthorised foreign aircraft found in Britain's airspace was liable to be fired at. Unlike Germany, however, Britain lacked an effective long-range anti-airship gun

Below: Clyne Woods, Swansea, scene of an impressive scareship sighting in January 1913

many argued that the act was like a dog with a loud bark, but with no teeth to bite with. It was against this background of events that a new wave of phantom airship sightings began in January 1913.

Early in the morning of 4 January three witnesses, including a police constable, saw and heard an airship flying over Dover. It came from the direction of the sea and disappeared from sight to the north east. Despite a strong westerly wind, the craft, which displayed a light and made a distinct droning sound, flew at a great speed. In this case it was alleged that a French airship from a base at Verdun, 120 miles (200 kilometres) away, had been the culprit, though it is hard to imagine why the craft would have made such a perilous journey at such an early hour in poor weather conditions.

Another significant sighting was made by Captain Lionel Lindsay, Chief Constable of Glamorganshire, on 17 January. At 4.45 p.m. he saw an airship pass over Cardiff. He said:

It was much bigger and moved faster than the Willows airship and left in its trail a dense volume of smoke. I called the attention of a bystander to the object, and he agreed with me that it was some large aircraft. It disappeared quickly so giving evidence of speedy movement.

Steven Morgan, of Merthyr, saw a similar object from his bedroom window, half an hour after Captain Lindsay. He was also impressed by the trail of smoke the airship left behind it. Before he could obtain the use of a powerful telescope the craft went out of view over the Aberdare Valley.

These sightings encouraged more witnesses to come forward. One such observer was a postman from Sketty, Swansea, who saw what looked like a very bright light hovering over Clyne Woods on 21 January at 7 p.m. Four days later, a mysterious aircraft going at a speed of 25 miles per hour (40 km/h) was seen by several people in Liverpool. Although members of a local flying club had been in the air earlier in the day, they said that at the time of the sighting it had been too windy for an extended flight. On several nights at the end of January many witnesses reported seeing a bright light moving over Manchester, which puzzled them.

Epidemic 'airshipitis'

The sightings of the airship, or airships, spread throughout the land to such an extent that a newspaper nicknamed the epidemic of reports 'airshipitis'.

When MP Mr Joynson-Hicks was asked about Captain Lindsay's sighting, he replied:

I don't doubt the report at all, for though our own aircraft can only do thirty or forty miles [50 or 65 kilometres], the Zeppelin vessels can cross the Channel. I believe, in fact, that foreign dirigibles are crossing the English Channel at will. It is a very serious matter.

Yorkshire became a new focal point for the sightings in February. Two young people in Scarborough were the first to see anything unusual in the night sky. At some time early in the month, Mr Taylor and Miss Hollings saw a light hovering over Scarborough racecourse. They were attracted by the sound of

machinery, which they attributed to the light. After a few minutes a conical beam of white light descended from the craft and was played upon the racecourse for six or seven minutes. The beam of light vanished and then reappeared briefly before the thing flew away towards Selby.

Another Yorkshire sighting occurred on 21 February, between 9 and 9.30 p.m., when two men on the sand barge *Star* were dredging the river Ouse at Beningborough, and saw a light in the sky. One of the witnesses, Mr Riply, said: 'It went round and round and then stopped. It stood stationary for a short time, and then went over Billington Locks. It stood there again for some time, and then went round and round as if surveying the country.' It repeated this activity several times before finally disappearing.

At the same time in Selby, a solicitor named Mr March saw from his home a bright star over Hambleton. The star moved up and down, and backwards and forwards, as if surveying the area, or looking for something. After 45 minutes it rapidly sailed towards Leeds.

It seems that 21 February must have been a busy night for the crew of the airship – if there was, indeed, only one – for not only did many people throughout Yorkshire report seeing its lights and hearing its motors, but it was also seen over Exhall, Warwickshire and

A spectacular airship was seen by two men who were dredging the river Ouse at Beningborough, Yorkshire, between 9.00 and 9.30 p.m. on 21 February 1913. The men saw the same airship again close by at 4 a.m. the next day, and kept it under observation for around an hour and a half

Hunstanton, Norfolk.

It was at this stage in the proceedings that the War Office began to take an interest in the sighting reports, and efforts were made to discover the identity of the mystery airship; the results of their investigations were, however, never disclosed.

Hundreds of sightings were made at the end of February by people throughout the United Kingdom. Many of these observations were, however, explained as visions of Venus, or balloons sent up by jokers. This was, indeed, true in many instances.

An impressive sighting that was not so easily explained was made by Captain Lundie and his crew aboard the *City of Leeds* steamer on 22 February at 9.15 p.m. As they were leaving the mouth of the Humber they saw high over the Yorkshire coast something that 'resembled a shark in appearance', said the captain. 'It had wings on either side, and we saw the tail of the machine. No lights were visible, but owing to the rays of the moon these were not necessary. . . . We had it under observation for about five minutes. It maintained a high altitude all the time, and finally disappeared over Grimsby.'

Mystery biplane

An intriguing sighting, possibly connected with the 'scareship' incidents, was made by a Mr Collins on board his yacht in Killary Harbour, Ireland. In late February he heard a droning sound above the bay, and saw an aeroplane coming from the direction of the sea. Suddenly it descended and landed inland. Mr Collins said:

I ran to shore thinking they might want help or information, as it might be a breakdown. I saw it was of the bi-plane type. The occupants were three in number, and one apparently a mechanic whom I could not see, tinkering at the engines. the other two were foreigners pretty stout, with florid complexions, and very intelligent foreheads, apparently Germans.

When he asked them, in German, if he could help them, one of the men answered him in French saying he did not understand, and then brusquely told him to go away as they had everything under control. Mr Collins did not see the aircraft take off again, but he did see a steamer on the horizon, which appeared to be waiting for the return of the aircraft and its impolite aeronauts.

The sheer number of sightings made in the beginning of 1913 makes this wave difficult to research and analyse, especially since there are nearly as many explanations put forward by the pundits of the period. However, mystery still shrouds many of these sightings, though UFO researchers have made a determined effort to come to terms with this material. The result of these researches should have interesting implications for modern-day UFO studies, when the data is finally collated.

UFOs and the digital computer

Computer processing of photographs of UFOs creates striking and bizarre images, while revealing subtleties that are difficult to discern in the originals. WILLIAM H. SPAULDING, director of Ground Saucer Watch, explains this new research technique

MOST PHOTOGRAPHS of unidentified flying objects are disappointing. They are blurred, lacking in detail and uninformative at a casual glance. Often they lack the context of landscape or everyday objects that would enable one to judge the size and distance of the UFOs. The few that are sharp and clear usually turn out to be fakes.

It is the task of the UFO photo analyst to sift through this mass of low-grade material, weed out the frauds and the misidentified aircraft, birds and astronomical objects, and call attention to the small residue of photographs that resist all attempts at being explained away.

Traditionally, UFO photo analysts have been limited to a few techniques of study. By measuring shadows they may be able to show that the picture consists of a landscape shot

Top: a swirl of vivid hues is a 'computer eye view' of a glowing disc seen over Colorado, USA (inset). The colours represent different brightness levels in the original image and forcefully portray detailed structure in the UFO and surrounding sky. The lines on the coloured image are 'drawn' by the computer as it makes measurements on the picture

combined with a picture of a model taken under totally different lighting conditions. By studying the focus on the UFO they may be able to show that it is much closer to the camera than the witness claimed, and is therefore much smaller than it appears. By enlarging details they may be able to reveal the presence of a tell-tale 'Frisbee' trade mark. More frequently they can identify the shot as showing some natural object – even that sceptics' favourite, the planet Venus, seen under unusual atmospheric conditions.

But all too often the label 'unidentified' has remained on the photograph because there was apparently too little information to resolve the question 'What is this mysterious object in the sky?' Yet even in the fuzziest photograph there are many subtle clues hidden away. Now a powerful new tool, the computer, promises to disclose them.

One UFO investigation group, Ground Saucer Watch, has applied the computer to the analysis of UFO photographs on a large scale. Ground Saucer Watch was founded in Cleveland, Ohio, USA, in 1957 in order to bring a high level of technical expertise to the study of UFO reports. The group wanted, in the words of a statement made then, to 'see positive scientific action taken to end the elements of foul-up and cover-up in UFO research'. A network of 500 scientific and engineering consultants assists it in this task.

Now the computer is available as an aid. It enabled Ground Saucer Watch, in a study of 1000 photographs that had *prima facie* plausibility, to reject all but 45 as misidentifications or hoaxes. Here are some of the techniques that are used to sift such quantities of material.

The pictures were analysed with a Computer Eye, manufactured by Spatial Data Systems, Inc. It uses a television-type camera that scans a picture and breaks it down into nearly a quarter of a million tiny 'pixels' (picture cells), in an array consisting of 512 columns and 480 rows.

Although the colours of the photographs provide important information, they do not come into our computer analyses. The scanner 'sees' only a black and white picture. The scanner measures the brightness of each pixel and assigns it a rating on a 'grey scale' from 0 (completely dark) to 31 (bright white). So the whole picture is reduced to a quarter of a million numbers, which are stored in the computer's memory. They can be recalled and used to build up a black and white image, a direct copy of the original, on a television screen linked to the computer. But they can also be manipulated in countless different ways to generate new images,

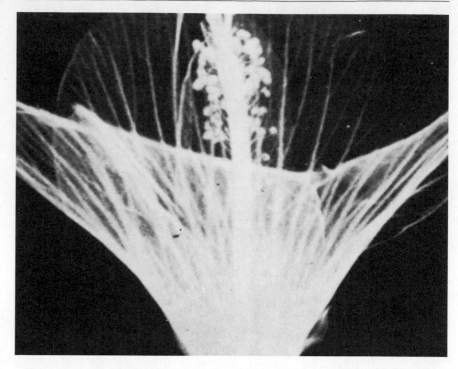

Above: an x-ray photograph of a flower. Lighter areas represent thicker tissues, which absorb x-rays more strongly than the thinner areas. Careful study is needed to see the details

Below: a computer-processed version of the picture above, in which edges separating light and dark areas have been enhanced. Some UFO pictures can be similarly clarified

which reveal unsuspected information in the original picture, or display it in unfamiliar and striking ways.

At the touch of a button the computer operator can do most of the things that the photo technician can do only at the cost of several hours' work in his laboratory.

The computer can instantly enlarge any selected detail of the picture to full-screen size. There are limits to the degree to which this can usefully be done. The picture becomes coarser as the mosaic of pixels becomes more evident. This begins to happen when the picture has been enlarged by about four times, in height and breadth.

The computer can 'stretch' the contrast, brightening the light areas and darkening the shadows, so emphasising the detail in a murky original. (This is what you do to your television picture when you turn up the contrast control.)

Enhancing the image

Measurements of distances and angles on the image become extremely easy. Crossed lines can be superimposed on the picture and moved at will, to identify points of interest. The computer can measure the positions of those points and instantly calculate distances and angles.

All this makes life easier for photo analysts, and enables them to plough through much more material than before. But the computer can also easily accomplish a number of feats that are impracticable, or even impossible, for the photo technician to perform.

For example, the computer can enhance the edges of the features seen in a photo. The effect of edge enhancement is illustrated here with a picture that is a little more conventional than a UFO photo. The x-ray picture of

a flower is in black and white. Each shade of grey carries information about the flower – its thickness, and hence ability to absorb x-rays, at that point. In this negative image, the brighter areas correspond to thicker areas of plant tissue. There is a great deal of delicate structure to be seen in the petals and the central pistil.

But the eye's ability to distinguish shades of grey is limited. The result obtained when the edges are enhanced is also shown opposite. Areas of uniform shade in the original are represented as a medium grey in the computer-processed picture. Wherever the original increases in lightness (from left to right) the computer draws a bright line, while where there is a transition from light to dark it draws a dark line. The result is arresting. The flower's structure, which was lost in the subtle, veil-like x-ray image, is now laid bare in a tracery of metallic clarity.

Edge enhancement has little relevance to the indistinct forms visible in many UFO pictures. However, it is revealing when applied to UFO images showing faint detail;

Like an artist with a taste for poster paints, the computer has transformed the x-ray flower picture on the opposite page into a bold pattern of colours. All the detail below is present in the original picture, but is now presented in a form that is more easily 'read' by the human eye and brain

these are generally dark objects seen against the daytime sky (see page 66). But another technique, colour coding, can extract information from the brightness pattern in the original pictures. It exploits the fact that the eye can distinguish colours far more readily than it can distinguish shades of grey.

To colour-code a picture, the computer is linked to a colour television set. Each pixel is assigned a colour according to its brightness. Thus, in the x-ray picture of the flower, the darkest areas are shown as black. The darkest shades of grey (the thinnest parts of the flower) are rendered as shades of violet and red. Increasingly light areas are shown as shades of yellow, green and blue. The lightest areas (the thickest parts of the plant) are rendered as white.

The result is a gaudier flower than nature has ever created, with all the details of structure leaping out at the eye. Radiographers use this type of colour coding on x-ray pictures to improve their view of the interior of the human body.

Astronomers and space engineers apply the same techniques to the photos they take with ground-based telescopes, and to the television images sent back from space satellites and probes. In the original picture, brightness levels may represent the actual brightness of a planet's surface, or the temperature of a gas cloud in space, or the intensity of radio waves from distant galaxies. The patterns in the computer-generated image will represent this information in terms of colour. So, though there is a superficial resemblance in these different types of picture, the information they give is totally different in nature.

An ambiguous message

What does the procedure reveal specifically about UFOs? The brightness pattern of light and dark in the photo image of a UFO is a complex and ambiguous 'message', involving the shape of the object, the amount of light it may be emitting at each point, its intrinsic lightness or darkness if it is being seen by reflected light, the effects of glare and atmospheric haze, and so on. Emphasising the pattern by the colour-coding technique often reveals the true form of the object immediately. A broken, uneven density may indicate a cloud. A cylindrical shape with protruberances may appear, indicating an aircraft body and wings partly hidden by glare. The contours of a 'daylight disc' (meaning any daytime UFO) are revealed, and often turn out to be suspiciously like those of a camera lens cap, a pie plate, or a hub cap.

Ground Saucer Watch has employed these techniques on thousands of photographs. Take as an example the two famous 'Colorado pictures' overleaf. They show single UFO sighted and photographed precisely 6.20 a.m. local time on 28 A 1969 by Mr Norman Vedaa and senger while driving north-east

Route 80S, approximately 70 miles (110 kilometres) east of Denver, Colorado. Mr Vedaa described the object as yellow-gold, tremendously brilliant, oval in shape, and soundless. He said: 'The object was bright, hard to look at – and appeared to hover momentarily. The object's glow . . . was producing a reflective light on the clouds below. . . .' Two colour transparencies were taken and do indeed show a bright yellowish glow with well-defined edges, back-lighting the clouds.

The colour-coding technique was used on the Colorado photographs, and the result is reproduced on page 61. Again, lighter parts of the original are represented by white, blue and yellow, while darker parts are represented by red, violet and black.

The light vertical lines in that picture and in the one below are just a different way of showing brightness information. The computer has taken a 'slice' down the picture along the left-hand line. At the right, it has plotted a graph of the brightness of the scene along that line, shown by the fluctuating line. Thus the 'bump' in the wavy line represents the bright centre of the object.

The computer also speeds up the detailed study of light and shadow at any selected region of the picture. Ground Saucer Watch has a 'library' of data on the proportion of light that is reflected by each of a large range of materials. In some photographs of UFOS seen by reflected daylight, everyday objects, such as trees or houses, are visible, with which the UFO image can be compared. This

Top: a tantalising glimpse of a UFO. An American motorist, Norman Vedaa, saw a brilliant disc and stopped his car to photograph it. It is visible near the top centre. The second picture (above) was taken within a few seconds, and was the original of the processed UFO images elsewhere in this article. The disc flew off at high speed

Right: measurements of image brightness made by the computer. The measurements are made along the left-hand line. The fluctuating line at the right shows the brightness: it curves to the right where the photograph is brightest. The curve helped to prove the disc was not a lens flare, weather balloon or aircraft

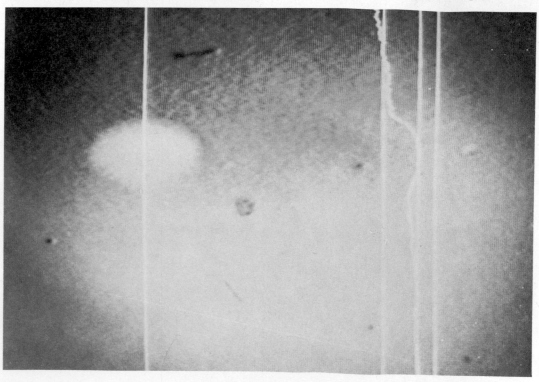

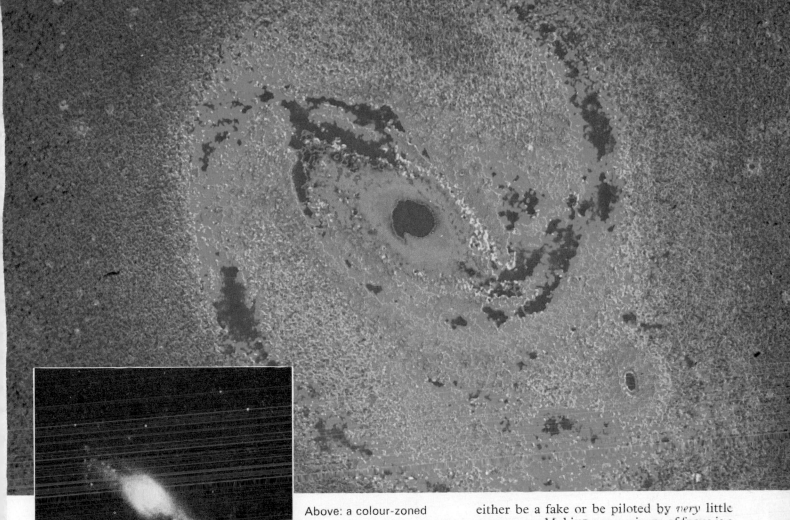

may enable the analyst to make a tentative judgement about the composition of the UFO.

We can compare the contrast in the light and shadowed areas of the UFO image and in landscape features: if there is a serious discrepancy, a composite picture or a model close to the camera is indicated. Essentially the same method can be used to estimate the degree to which atmospheric haze veils the UFO image. The more distant the object is, the lighter and less contrasty it will appear because of light scattered by air molecules, dust and water vapour. This often allows us to make an estimate of the distance of the UFO from the witness.

Careful measurements on the sharpness of various features in the picture are also a valuable indicator of distance. In fact, the annoying fuzziness of most UFO pictures – which are no worse than most holiday snaps in this respect – can be turned to advantage.

Sometimes the image of a UFO in the sky is beautifully sharp, while all ground features more than 50 feet (15 metres) away are slightly out of focus. This shows that the object is close to the camera – and so must

Above: a colour-zoned image of a giant star system reveals the detail latent in a black and white picture (left), itself the computerised average of five photographs. The galaxy, a mass of billions of stars and vast quantities of gas and dust swirling in a spiral, is 40 million light years from us. The coloured image shows its spiral arms extending as far as its companion elliptical galaxy at lower right. Further image processing revealed extraordinary ray-like structures surrounding the spiral galaxy. Astronomers realise the value of the computer in extracting information from their photographs. Scientific UFO study may benefit equally

either be a fake or be piloted by very little green men. Making comparisons of focus is a traditional part of UFO photo analysis, now greatly facilitated by the computer.

In its study of the Vedaa pictures, Ground Saucer Watch was able to rule out more and more explanations that seek to reduce the sightings to causes that are well-known and understood. This was no weather balloon, flock of birds or daylight meteor – the brightness distribution was that of a disc. It was not an aircraft hidden in the glare of reflected sunlight – it was too bright for that, and not a trace of tail or wings could be found. Lens flares, reflections from clouds, mirages and other atmospheric effects are all ruled out: the Sun is in the wrong position for them. The object was three-dimensional in form, and it was certainly a long way from the camera.

Objective research will progress with the aid of modern technology, of which the computer is an important component. In the near future photo analysis will be carried out by more sophisticated computer programming, in conjunction with more powerful 'hardware' – faster computers with bigger memory capacity, working with scanners that can break the original image down into yet finer detail. Soon it will become virtually impossible to fake a UFO photograph. Then, perhaps, the UFO mystery will be solved.

Analysing the Trent photos

Computer analysis lends support to two of the best known UFO photographs. This chapter describes the studies carried out on these classic pictures – and suggests that the US government has for years sown confusion about UFOS

Above: a huge disc glides silently across the sky over the small Trent farm in Oregon, USA, and is captured in one of the most famous UFO photographs

Above: one of the Trents' pictures of the mysterious object shows its disc-shaped outline. In the Trents' words: 'The object was coming in toward us and seemed to be tipped up a little bit. It was very bright – almost silvery – and there was no noise or smoke'

THE COMPUTER HAS BEEN USED to analyse two of the most impressive UFO photographs to date, taken by an American couple, Mr and Mrs Trent, near McMinnville, Oregon, USA. The computer study has endorsed and extended the findings of the expert appointed by the University of Colorado's Condon Committee – that the pictures show an object that is not explicable as any known phenomenon, natural or artificial.

By the Trents' own account, the object appeared over their small farm in the early part of the evening on 11 May 1950. It was seen by Mrs Trent as she fed the farm's rabbits, and she called her husband. The family camera was found, and Mrs Trent took two photographs from positions a few feet apart. There was no sound as the disc glided from the north-eastern part of the sky across to the north-west.

There were a few unused frames left on the roll of film. The Trents attached so little importance to the pictures that they waited a few days, until they had used up the rest of the film, before they had the roll developed. They then ignored the photographs and it

was only by chance that the local newspaper heard about them. When they did, however, the pictures caused a sensation, finally being featured in *Life* magazine. They were the only photographs that were not dismissed by the US Air Force's highly sceptical Condon report of 1967, which was scathing about the mass of evidence presented to it. Their investigator, William K. Hartmann, concluded that all the factors he had investigated, both in the photographs and at the scene of the sighting, were consistent with the assertion 'that an extraordinary flying object, silvery, metallic, disc-shaped, tens of metres in diameter, and evidently artificial, flew within sight of two witnesses'. The evidence, he said, did not positively rule out a hoax – which, coming from a member of the Condon team, almost rates as an endorsement of authenticity.

Controversy blew up around these photos, however, as it does around all UFO pictures that stand up to scrutiny (see box). The advent of the computer afforded an opportunity to review the Trent photographs in order to discover more than the human eye can see, even when it is aided by the microscope.

The principles involved in the computer study techniques used to analyse the photographs have already been described (see page 61). A television camera scans the picture, breaking it down into nearly a quarter of a million pixels (picture cells) and recording the lightness or darkness of each pixel as a number stored in its memory. The computer can process these numbers in countless different ways to create new images, which it displays on a television screen. Each such picture has something new to say about the information contained in the original photographic negative.

Colour-contouring the image

The first thing that Ground Saucer Watch, the investigating organisation, did with the Trent photos was to colour-contour the image, converting each shade of grey in the original picture into a different bright colour. The result was to make the distribution of light and shade over the object far easier to 'read'.

The lower surface of the disc shows only a few different shades, confirming an evenly lit, flat lower surface. The second photograph, showing the edge-on disc, disclosed a darker shade in the centre of the object than at the extreme edges, which indicates a circular shape and bevelled disc profile.

The colour-coding technique makes the light-and-shade pattern of the image plainly visible to the eye. Detailed calculations by the computer provide a more sophisticated judgement confirming the detailed shape of the object shown.

Hoax photographs generally show such items as hub caps or dishes, but the obvious

Below: a computerised view of the disc seen in the Trent photographs. Each shade of grey in the original has been turned into a particular colour, making the details in the picture easier to 'read'. The object is seen to have a flat, evenly lit underside

shapes of such objects would be resolved by the colour-contouring technique applied to the magnified image.

The computer technicians measured the lightness of the UFO image and compared it with the shadows that can be seen on the nearby garage. The UFO turned out to be much lighter. The most straightforward explanation of this effect is that the object is at a great distance from the camera. Atmospheric haze over that distance would veil the disc – just as an observer, looking at the distant horizon, finds that it looks paler than nearby foreground objects, even on days when the air is at its clearest. However, other possible factors, including reflected ground light and grease on the camera lens, have been brought into the controversy. But this objection cannot be brought against the estimation of the object's distance by means of the sharpness of the UFO image. The foreground objects, such as the telephone wires and the building, are sharper than the UFO and distant objects on the ground.

The next step in the analysis was to search for wires suspending or supporting the disc, which would imply that the object was a small model, comparatively close to the camera. To

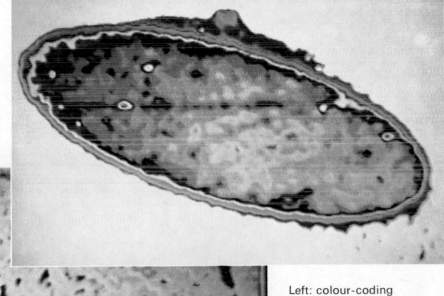

Left: colour-coding emphasises the form shown in the side-on view of the object. This wingless disc, with its curious off-centre tower, is unlike any known man-made aircraft

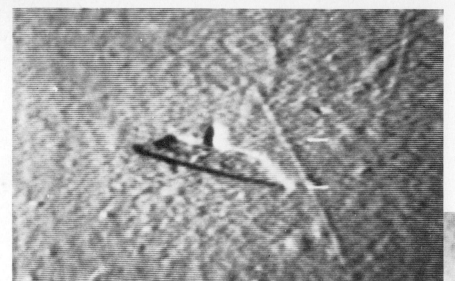

have long asserted that the United States intelligence agencies are aware of the existence and origins of UFOs. For more than 25 years they have maintained that the government knew more than it was telling. On numerous occasions when the government became involved in the investigation of a sighting, evidence would mysteriously disappear or be destroyed. The computer and other modern aids to analysis cannot demonstrate their full potential while vital evidence is withheld.

However, the Freedom of Information Act now gives American citizens powers to

do this, the group took advantage of the edge-enhancement facility of the computer.

The resulting pictures have something of the look of a bas-relief carved in rough stone and lit at a low angle. Bright and dark lines now mark the edges of features on the object, and even small flaws in the negatives. The edge-enhancement technique can reveal, under typical conditions, the presence of a wire less than one hundredth of an inch (a quarter of a millimetre) thick, at a distance of 10 feet (3 metres). There is definitely no evidence of such a supporting wire or string in the area around the object.

The edge-enhancement technique not only ruled out the theory of a suspended model: it made it easy for Ground Saucer Watch to make measurements of the size of the image, which, when coupled with the analysts' assessment of the distance of the object, enabled them to draw conclusions about its true size.

Results of the analysis

The accumulated evidence gleaned from the several lines of attack that Ground Saucer Watch followed in its computer study led the organisation to the sober conclusion that the picture shows a flying disc, between 65 and 100 feet (20 and 30 metres) in diameter, and probably made of polished metal (since its light reflection was consistent with laboratory specimens of metal).

The entire UFO phenomenon deserves a properly conducted scientific investigation, undistorted by preconceived opinions. Modern technology has the means to make progress on the subject. However, there is a factor that impedes serious UFO research. Most governments have preferred to conceal the full extent of their own evidence from their citizens. The United States government probably has available to it the largest pool of data that exists anywhere in the world – data that have come from its own employees, military personnel, policemen and ordinary citizens. Civilian UFO researchers

The sceptics put their case

The Trent photographs have been scrutinised intently for three decades. The first scientific analyst, William K. Hartmann, studied the haze, apparently atmospheric, that veils the UFO, and decided the object was about 1400 yards (1.3 kilometres) distant. A sceptical analyst, Robert Sheaffer, claims the haze could be due to grease on the camera

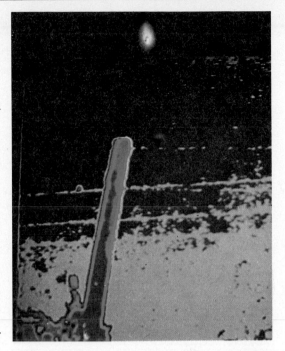

compel their government to disclose the information that its agencies hold on file. The first legal skirmishes have taken place and documents that the CIA would have preferred to keep to itself have been made available to ufologists.

It may prove, as more information is prised from unwilling hands, that the role of the US government has been more active than previously suspected – that the clouding of UFO investigation they have brought about is due to more than the usual torpor, confusion and conservatism of government departments. On the contrary, some small and as yet unidentified group within the government machine may have been manipulating public opinion and the work of ufologists. They could have done this by familiar techniques of 'disinformation' – releasing distorted reports and data, starting rumours, feeding ufologists with 'confidential' but misleading stories – even setting up the occasional spurious sighting. They would have done this to set up a background of widespread UFO belief – at the same time that other government agencies were busily debunking UFOs.

There could be several motives for such a devious strategy. Public attention has occasionally been distracted from other issues by well-timed 'saucer flaps'. For example, a wave of sightings over Texas and New Mexico occurred within hours of the news of the Soviet Union's launching of a second Sputnik in November 1957, at a time when America's Vanguard rockets were failing to get off the launch pad.

The long-running UFO story could also provide vast quantities of data on the psychology of individuals and groups as they found themselves under supposed surveillance by unknown and possibly threatening forces. The official interest in the psychological warfare aspects of UFO scares is documented in secret memoranda only now becoming available.

The plethora of sightings that has grown up during the last 30 years could also serve to bury the occasional sighting of advanced types of aircraft by citizens or unauthorised service personnel.

A UFO tradition

An agency wishing to foment a UFO tradition and the occasional outbreak of UFO hysteria would not need to do a great deal. The enthusiasts and the general public would do it for them, at the stimulus of a few hints, added to the UFO reports made in good faith. Better analysis of UFO data of all kinds, in which computerised image-processing has a large part to play, can improve the situation by countering such a campaign and combatting the extremes of credulity and scepticism. But for this all the evidence hidden in government files is needed.

So, while Ground Saucer Watch adheres firmly to its judgement that remarkable physical phenomena lie behind many of the UFO photographs, it believes that the battle to discover the true nature and origin of those phenomena may be fought out in the courtroom before it can be taken up in the photo analyst's laboratory.

Left: the edges of the features visible in the two Trent photographs are enhanced in these two computer-generated images. Scratches and other blemishes on the ill-treated negatives are clearly brought out – but there is no trace of the wire that would be expected if the object were a model suspended from the telephone wires overhead

Right: colour-coded detail from one of the Trent photographs. The focus of the telephone pole seen here, and of other objects in the pictures was studied and compared with the focus of the disc images. The comparison indicated that the disc was too far from the camera to be a model

Below left: the puzzling garage shadows, clarified by colour-contouring

Left: during an investigation, William K. Hartmann tries to fake a UFO by a means of a small suspended model

Below: Philip J. Klass, who attacks the authenticity of the Trent photographs

lens, and the object could be close to the camera. He also points out that shadows of the garage eaves appear on the wall in the picture; but this wall faces east, suggesting the photograph was taken in the early morning, not the evening as the Trents claimed. The UFO sceptic Philip J. Klass suggests a motive for falsifying the time of the event: a morning sighting would be implausible since local farmers would be in the fields and it would be surprising that none of them had seen the UFO. Another investigator, Bruce Maccabee, replies that the garage shadows indicate a diffuse light source, probably a bright cloud illuminated by the evening Sun. He has calculated the UFO to be over 1000 yards (1 kilometre) away, even allowing for lens grease. Klass also asserts that the shift in UFO direction between the pictures exactly equals what would be expected if it were a stationary model suspended close to the camera. While Klass points out that the Trents have shown reluctance to take lie-detector tests, Maccabee and other investigators insist on the transparent sincerity of the couple in all interviews. The experts seem unable to dispel the dust they themselves have raised, and the controversy will continue.

UFO photos: facts and frauds

Nine out of ten photographs of alleged UFOs are misinterpreted pictures of everyday events or are the work of hoaxers. ROBERT S. DIGBY, of the British UFO Research Association, and CHRIS COOPER describe the gauntlet of tests that such photos must run

WELL-TRIED METHODS of analysing and evaluating UFO photographs will be supplemented, but not superseded, by newer methods of image-processing by computer. In fact the more sophisticated and expensive techniques of analysis are generally reserved for photographs that have survived the more traditional examination. These are a small minority of all claimed UFO pictures. At most, 10 per cent of the photographs that analysts study still seem convincing after they have been exposed to a battery of tests.

A UFO photograph is a report like any other, and requires to be supported in the same way. Many pictures that seem to be authentic cannot be used as evidence for the occurrence of some inexplicable phenomenon simply because of the unsatisfactory circumstances of the sighting. The photographer may have been alone at the time, for example; however strongly a researcher might be convinced of the sincerity of the witness, sceptics can hardly be blamed for insisting on the possibility of a hoax.

Inducements for hoaxers

Financial motives for creating a successful hoax photograph are very strong. One person who took photographs allegedly showing the Loch Ness monster refused to release the negatives for study by experts. Despite this and the fact that there are inconsistencies in his account of the sighting, his photographs were prominently featured in the British press and continue to be used. He has commented that the use of the pictures by the media all over the world would fetch something like £200,000 over the first six months. Income would continue long after that, of course, and there would also be fees for lectures and personal appearances. There are great incentives for providing what the public wants to see.

Among some people, especially bright schoolchildren, it has become a hobby to fake 'flying saucer' photographs. One of the best-known cases is that of Alex Birch, which took place in Britain. In 1962, when Alex was a 14-year-old schoolboy, he produced a photograph of a group of five saucer-like objects. He was interviewed on radio and television and by the Air Ministry. He appeared before the inaugural meeting of the British UFO

Above: UFO hoaxster Alex Birch revealing how he faked a picture of 'flying saucers' that had been accepted as real ever since he took it, 10 years before he made his confession

Above right: the 'daylight discs' that Alex Birch, then 14 years old, claimed to have photographed as they passed over Sheffield, in northern England, in 1962. The shapes were actually painted on the windowpane through which he took the photograph

Right: one of many pictures of flying discs taken in New Mexico by Paul Villa, who claimed to have talked with their crews. Computer studies indicated that the pictures showed small models

Research Association to explain the circumstances of his sighting. It was only 10 years later that his plausible, tenaciously defended and apparently sincere story was admitted to be a hoax.

Hence the vital importance of having independent witnesses to a sighting. The ideal case, from the investigator's viewpoint, is one in which the witnesses are neither friends nor relatives of the photographer, and make full statements of the circumstances of the sighting before the film has been processed. Hoaxers are rarely bold enough to announce their 'sightings' before they have made quite sure that their pictures are sufficiently convincing.

Hard evidence

So the first requirement for a photograph if it is to provide 'hard' scientific evidence is that there should be at least one other witness, who is independent of the photographer. The second requirement is that the original film – whether it is a black and white negative, a colour negative or a colour transparency – be submitted to qualified analysts for examination and evaluation. The whole film roll should be provided, even if only one or two frames show the UFO image. The other pictures may provide valuable evidence about the weather conditions, whether there was grease or dirt on the lens, whether there was stray light in the camera, the characteristics of that particular sample of film, and much else besides.

The third requirement is that there should be reference points in the picture. If it shows an object against a blank sky and nothing more, distance and size cannot be calculated.

The fourth requirement is not obligatory, but it is highly desirable: that there should be a sequence of pictures. A series of still photographs provides more information than a single one could; and a movie sequence is still more valuable. A movie film is harder to fake than a still photograph, and it provides information about the time elapsed during the sighting. (On some cameras the speed of the film can be varied from the normal 24 frames per second. It is essential that the witness report should specify what speed was used during the filming of the UFO.)

The UFO investigator presented with a photograph will also want to know full details of the camera and film used, the distance, aperture and speed settings, whether there was a filter over the lens and if so, of what type it was, whether the camera was hand-held or tripod-mounted, and any other information that might be relevant.

So a great deal of the investigator's work is done before he or she gets down to a detailed study of the picture. What needs to be done when that analysis at last begins?

The University of Colorado was given a contract in 1966 to study UFOs on behalf of the US Air Force. Many UFO investigators have been sceptical of the value of the report that was finally published under the title *The scientific study of unidentified flying objects*,

Below: a small, near object can produce a photographic image of the same size as a large object farther away. The true size can be calculated if its distance can be determined – for example, by analysis of its sharpness of focus

Bottom: an orbiting 'saucer' photographed from the spacecraft *Aurora 7* in May 1962. This ambiguous image could have fuelled endless speculation about alien observation of human space activity if Scott Carpenter, who took the picture, had not known its true nature: a small clump of ice crystals that had detached themselves when he knocked the side of the craft

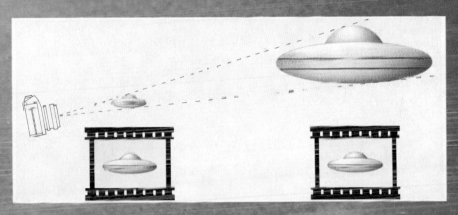

however, the approach that photographic evidence requires was clearly outlined by the Colorado investigators, and can provide a good guide to other analysts. This approach falls into several phases:

Firstly there is a subjective evaluation. Do various photographic factors such as clarity and contrast, combined with the witnesses' testimony, make the picture appear both plausible and informative about a potentially unusual phenomenon?

If a photograph passes this initial qualitative assessment, the second phase of investigation asks whether there is any rational explanation for what is shown in the picture. This question can be tackled only by someone who has wide experience with astronomical, meteorological, optical and photographic effects. Only such a person is equipped to know the surprising forms that can be assumed by aircraft vapour trails, stars and planets seen under unusual atmospheric conditions, lens flares, faulty film processing and countless other straightforward but poorly appreciated effects. Yet such possible causes of a 'UFO' image are so infinitely diverse that even the expert will be fooled on occasion. Nevertheless many photographs will be rejected at this stage of examination as cases of mistaken interpretation.

In the third phase of investigation the possibility of a fake is examined. Even with the best credentials concerning the sincerity of the report, this possibility remains and must be tested by the investigator. Are there any signs of tampering with the original film? Such interference can usually be detected. An elementary question to ask is: do the frames represent a continuous sequence? If the manufacturer's frame numbers reveal that the available pictures are separated by

Top: when was the UFO photographed? A hypothetical picture like this has many clues for the analyst. The relation between the height of the telephone poles and the length of their shadows shows that the elevation of the Sun is 38° (centre). An on-the-spot study of the direction of the shadows in relation to landmarks reveals the direction of the Sun (above) as 8° south of east. From this, and the latitude of the site, the date and time at which the picture was taken can be calculated

others, which the witness cannot or will not make available, the suspicion arises that the shots do not belong to a single sighting but were 'set up' on separate occasions – or else that obviously unconvincing shots have been deliberately withheld.

Are the focus, sharpness and contrast in accord with the description by the photographer and others? If the object is alleged to have sped across the sky there should be some corresponding degree of blurring in the UFO image – or, if the photographer panned while taking the shot, there should be some blurring of the landscape.

The focus of the image can provide an accurate estimate of the distance of the object. This is crucial to a judgement of the authenticity of a photograph, since most hoaxes involve small objects positioned close to the camera. Nevertheless, even if the UFO image is judged to be distant from the camera, the possibility remains that the witness knows it to be an everyday object, such as an aeroplane at an unusual angle, but has decided to cash in on the peculiarity of its appearance in the picture.

Clues from lighting conditions

Further tests of consistency between the pictures and the witnesses' testimony can be made. In daytime photographs, angles of sunlight and weather conditions can be checked to see whether they agree with the stated time and date of occurrence of the sighting. If the height of an object appearing in the picture and the length of its shadow can both be measured, the height of the Sun can immediately be calculated, and by the use of an astronomical *ephemeris* or nautical almanac the time of day can be found. The local weather office will have detailed records of the weather on that day. Not only might they confirm or contradict the time of the alleged sighting, but such information as the height of the cloud base can, in some circumstances, give information about the height of the object photographed.

Study of the lighting conditions may also show whether the photographs in a sequence have been taken within a short period of each other. If a sighting is described as having lasted a few seconds, and the Sun is found to have moved through, say, 10 degrees between one shot and another – corresponding to 40 minutes – then the credibility of the witnesses is destroyed.

This investigation may very well be carried on to an examination of the camera itself, if this is available. The true shutter speeds and apertures of most cameras can be substantially different from their nominal values and it can be vital to obtain an accurate value.

It is also highly desirable to visit the scene of the sighting. The purpose of this is generally not to look for physical traces of the UFO – though such evidence, if available, is invaluable – but to make measurements to determine the sizes and directions of objects

Left: a spherical UFO hovers over the city of New York – or so it seems. The picture was taken by civil defence observers as they watched a 'round orange light' drift over the city. But the 'globe' has been judged to be a lens flare, formed coincidentally

Below: a large domed disc flew over the home of Ralph Ditter in Ohio, USA, in November 1966, according to his account. He took three Polaroid pictures during the $1\frac{1}{2}$ minutes of the sighting. Two came out – but the print allegedly taken first was actually taken later, according to the maker's numbers. And the interval between the pictures, as indicated by the shadows, was much greater than the reported $1\frac{1}{2}$ minutes

candidates – though it seems that controversy concerning such pictures never quite dies down. Some of the most convincing photographs are the stills taken aboard a Brazilian naval ship participating in scientific studies as part of the International Geophysical Year. At 12.15 p.m. on 16 January 1958, while the ship was off Trindade Island in the South Atlantic, large numbers of personnel on the deck of the ship saw a strange object approach the island at high speed, hover over it for a while, disappear behind a peak, reappear and head out to sea. Four photographs taken by Almiro Barauna, a civilian photographer on board at the time, show an object resembling two dishes face-to-face surrounded by a vapour or mist.

In many respects this was a near-perfect sighting. There were many witnesses and the negatives were developed immediately, virtually ruling out a fake.

The US Air Force later claimed they had made a detailed investigation and concluded that the affair was a hoax. However, their publicly available file does not contain any evaluation of the case. If they have any

that are visible in the picture.

Of the photographs that run this gauntlet of tests, few survive with their credibility intact. But when they do, the final classification is essentially of a negative kind – the object shown is not a nearby object, not a plane, not a meteor. Unfortunately the ideas often associated with the term 'UFO' – ideas of extra-terrestrial craft – cause misunderstanding between the public and serious-minded researchers. People ask, in all seriousness: 'Do UFOs exist?'. This is tantamount to asking whether anything has ever been seen in the skies that remains unidentified – and this is obviously so. The question that such enquirers really have in mind is: do alien spaceships visit the Earth? And to this we do not have an answer. No firm evidence exists that unambiguously shows the phenomena to be due to this cause.

We might ask, less ambitiously: are there any photographs that have resisted all attempts to discredit them? There are many

information throwing doubt on the pictures, they have kept it to themselves. There is no publicly available evidence against the authenticity of the Trindade Island photographs. The Brazilian investigators decided that the object seen in the pictures was 120 feet (36 metres) across and flying at 560 to 620 miles per hour (900 to 1000 km/h).

Equally remarkable objects are shown in many other photographs (see pages 61 and 66). But whether they are space visitors or something even more exotic, such as thought projections, cannot be discovered by photographic analysis alone.

Alien Contacts

Scientific attempts to make contact with intelligent life on other planets have so far been unsuccessful. But what of the evidence from people who claim to have met aliens? JENNY RANDLES examines their reports

ON A WET AND WINDY NIGHT in November 1980, Mario Luisi was walking through sodden meadows by a river outside his home village of Burneside in the English Lake District. In the darkness he saw what he took to be a cow. Then he thought it might be a crudely constructed sheep shelter. But then he saw that the object was hovering 3 feet (1 metre) above the ground and looked like nothing so much as a distorted aeroplane. It was about the size of a helicopter and had what seemed to be a tailplane, but no wings. It bore strange symbols, the like of which Luisi had never seen before.

As he stared at the weird object glinting in the beam of his lantern, he became aware of a squelching sound. He realised that someone was approaching him across the soggy ground and turned the beam of the lantern in the direction of the sound. He saw two figures, apparently human, about 6 feet (2 metres) away, beside an old oak tree. They were wearing dark, skin-tight suits. At that instant one of them, apparently female, raised a small pencil-shaped object in her hand. A bright light shot out from it, striking the face of Luisi's lantern. The glass front shattered and, as Luisi watched, the metal reflector became warped and twisted.

The remainder of Mario Luisi's encounter took place by the light from a paper mill on the other side of the river. The female figure spoke to him, telling him that she and

In this scene from Steven Spielberg's film *Close encounters of the third kind*, the protagonist enters a space-ship, surrounded by aliens who, although their only means of communication with human beings appears to be the repetition of a tune of five notes, are obviously benevolent. Despite its title, Spielberg's film deals with what UFO experts have labelled close encounters of the fourth kind – those in which there is intelligent contact with aliens

her companion meant no harm and had come to the Earth in peace. (Presumably, then, their 'attack' was a defensive measure against what they had taken to be a weapon – the lantern.) Luisi was told that he must not reveal the strange symbols on the ship, nor those on the lapel badges worn by both figures. He could only stare, his legs shaking, as the two beings, who were fair-skinned, entered their craft by means of a ladder that descended from it. Presently the object shot upwards, leaving a glow in the sky.

The encounter left Mario Luisi with a memory that would change his outlook on life. For him, at least, there was no longer any doubt – no need to question whether the human race is alone in the Universe. He 'knew' that we are not.

This problem has fascinated mankind ever since it was realised, in the 16th century, that the planets are other worlds, and the stars are other suns, possibly possessing their own planets. The human race seems to abhor the idea of being alone in an immeasurably vast Universe. This sentiment was exploited to great effect by Steven Spielberg's epic film *Close encounters of the third kind*, which was released in 1977. Spielberg brought the idea vividly to life. He himself is keenly interested in UFOs and is associated with the Center for UFO Studies, in Evanston, Illinois, USA, which is run by J. Allen Hynek, a consultant to *The Unexplained*.

The most fantastic type of evidence on the question consists of the numerous accounts of close encounters of the fourth kind – of which Mario Luisi's is one. These go beyond close encounters of the third kind, in which aliens are merely seen: witnesses claim to

Encounters of the fourth kind

have met, talked to, travelled in company with, or even been abducted by creatures not of this world.

Four varieties of close encounters of the fourth kind have been distinguished. Mario Luisi's experience is typical of type A, which embraces straightforward encounters where the witness fully remembers what took place. There are no memory blocks, no intervals of time that the subject is unable to recall, no obvious reason to doubt that the experience was of something completely real. It is just as much a part of the sequence of events as getting up that morning.

These type A events are the most sober evidence for the reality of aliens. And they are by no means rare. Although close encounters of the fourth kind as a whole make up no more than about 1 or 2 per cent of the total number of UFO reports made each year, this still amounts to many hundreds of cases since the Second World War. They come from almost every country and all social groups. And over half of these encounters are of type A. It is thought that they could be even more common than the figures suggest, for there is evidence that witnesses are unwilling to talk about this kind of experience.

Seeing an unidentified light in the sky is almost commonplace these days, and people are more willing to report it than they once were. But talking to a creature from another world is, for many people, something to keep quiet about. This is unfortunate, since it means that researchers are unsure of the true scale of the phenomenon. But the information supplied by courageous witnesses is sufficient to indicate that something truly extraordinary is going on.

But serious problems arise, even in these seemingly rational type A accounts. The Mario Luisi case is typical in this respect. He volunteered the lantern for scientific study. The results of two independent analyses were identical: in the opinion of experts the

damage was done by ordinary means, probably by a blow-torch. Had Luisi concocted his story and damaged the lantern himself, it would have been odd for him to be so co-operative. And it is not possible to disprove his claim, by which he stands, that the lantern was struck by a beam from an alien weapon.

Certain other points in Mario Luisi's story support his claims. But support is not proof, and we never do get proof in cases of close encounters of the fourth kind that a witness is not lying. The difficulty, of course, is that even if the witness is telling the truth, there is no guarantee that his alien contacts are not using materials and technology indistinguishable from our own. Nevertheless, when what is presented as evidence could perfectly well be of earthly origin, one is bound to become suspicious.

Science and the aliens

A number of researchers have been conducting studies into close encounters of the fourth kind, analysing the features of the stories in detail. Type A cases stand out from the other reports in many ways. They tend to occur outside the usual surroundings of the witness – in the open, perhaps in a field, and so on. They happen at any time of the day, even though UFOs are predominantly nocturnal. The average number of witnesses per case is well below the average for all UFO cases, but close to the average for all close encounters of the fourth kind.

Photographs purporting to show alien beings are, disappointingly, rare. This seems highly significant when it is remembered that UFO photographs are very numerous. If the

Previous page: two aliens allegedly visited a Lake District village one stormy November night in 1980. Disturbed by Mario Luisi on a night-time stroll, they apparently mistook his lamp for some kind of weapon, and destroyed it with a ray gun. Luisi later produced the damaged lamp as evidence (below) but expert analyses established that the damage could have been done with an ordinary blow-torch. On the other hand, there is no reason why an alien weapon should *not* have the same effect as a blow-torch!

Right: an analysis of UFO reports from the United Kingdom over the period from 1975 to 1979. Low definition cases are reports whose details are sparse, with only brightness, colour and movement clearly describable. Medium definition cases are those in which the object has a definite physical substance and shape. The remainder of cases are classified as close encounters (CEs). Close encounters of the fourth kind are, in turn, divided into four categories (far right)

number of pictures of aliens were in the same proportion as the number of contact cases – 1 or 2 per cent – then we would have a great deal of material to work on. In fact there are no more than two or three photographs and none that, beyond reasonable doubt, link an alien being with a UFO.

Yet we cannot complacently dismiss the phenomenon as unreal. For there are cases in which several witnesses see aliens. One example occurred on 3 March 1980, at Rio Pièdras, Puerto Rico. Two teenage children, Vivian and José Rodriguez, were woken at 3.30 a.m. by a barking dog. They looked through the window of their farm to see five strange creatures, with pointed ears and webbed feet, wearing tight-fitting clothes. The aliens seemed interested in the family's chickens. No UFO was observed by the children.

Next day it was discovered that at the same time of night two men nearby had seen the same creatures. The witnesses had been sleeping in a parked car, resting during a long journey. They had woken up and had seen a large domed object on the ground. Beings fitting the description given by the children had emerged from the object and headed in the direction of the Rodriguez farm.

Such a story, if true, is very hard to explain as anything other than a real, physical event. The apparent subjectivity of these type A cases should not be overstressed.

The second group of contact cases, type B, is quite different. The aliens involved are often called 'bedroom visitors' because so many of them make their appearance in the bedroom; the witnesses usually claim to have experienced the encounter while wide awake. These encounters have a good deal in common with ghost sightings that happen in the bedroom.

What distinguishes these events from type A cases is that they possess obvious distortions of reality – parts of the sequence of events are completely forgotten, there are jumps in the story from one scene of action to another, as in a film or a dream. The reality of the events is much more doubtful than that of the type A cases.

For example, on 5 January 1980 a 33-year-old house-painter awoke at 5 a.m. in his bedroom at Trowbridge, Wiltshire, in southern England. He saw a glowing green figure, 7 feet (2.1 metres) tall, at the foot of his bed. It looked more like a projected image

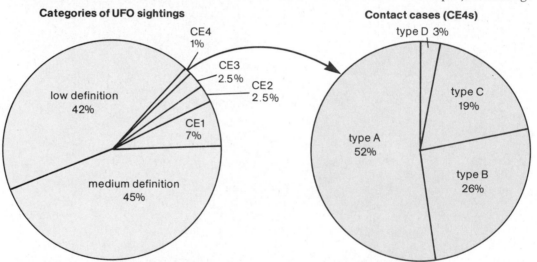

Categories of UFO sightings

- low definition 42%
- medium definition 45%
- CE1 7%
- CE2 2.5%
- CE3 2.5%
- CE4 1%

Contact cases (CE4s)

- type A 52%
- type B 26%
- type C 19%
- type D 3%

	non-contact UFO sightings	contact cases (CE4s)		
		type A	type B	type C
average number of witnesses	2.19	1.28	1.16	1.62
sex of witnesses	68% male	75% male	51% male	60% male
most common place of occurrence	home environment	in the open	room inside a building	in a car on a country road
most common time of occurrence	peak at about 9 p.m.	all times of day and night	peak at about 3 a.m.	peak at about 11 p.m.

This seems to suggest that the two types of contact are different in nature: type A sound like real contacts with something physical; type B sound like some kind of hallucination. It seems a plausible working hypothesis, though there are cases in which it is hard to decide whether a case belongs to type A or type B.

The third category of contact report, type C, involves an experience that is not immediately remembered. The experience of an English family, the Days, will illustrate how disturbing this can be.

Late-night encounter

One evening in October 1974, John and Sue Day were driving to their home at Aveley, in Essex. They had been visiting relatives and were now hurrying, hoping to catch a late-night television play. Their three children were with them and fell asleep during the journey. Then their parents saw a blue light pacing the car. They watched it for some time but were unable to identify what it could be.

Then the light disappeared – and the car turned a corner and ran into a well-defined bank of eerie green mist. The Days were in the mist for only a few seconds, but the car radio sparked and crackled. John instantly yanked out its wires to prevent a fire hazard. After recovering their composure the family drove the few hundred yards to their home.

When they got home they switched on their television set, but the screen remained blank. It was two hours later than they had

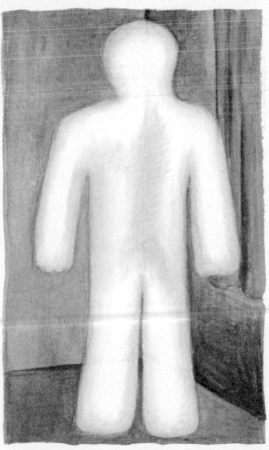

than a solid figure. The alien told the witness that the people to whom he belonged regularly shipped human beings off to other worlds in order to colonise them. When a planet became overcrowded they started a war in order to reduce the population. This behaviour seemed to be in conflict with other efforts that they were making to protect us: it seemed that our planet was liable to split in half and the alien visitors were desperately trying to plug the cracks by injecting a liquid cement from their remotely controlled space vehicles!

Interestingly, the witness's wife was in bed beside him all this time, yet she did not awaken, nor did it occur to him to disturb her. It seems most unlikely that anyone would make up such a story and expect anyone to believe it. It is not necessary to doubt the witness's sincerity – but neither is it necessary to take this weird story at all seriously.

Type B cases are rarer than type A – they form about a quarter of all contact reports. They are far more subjective, since they are almost exclusively single-witness encounters. By far the majority of them occur in the home or its immediate surroundings – fully two thirds of the cases occur in the bedroom. And most of them happen in the early hours of the morning.

Strange creatures with pointed ears and webbed feet seen examining chickens on a Puerto Rican farm on 3 March 1980 were also observed near their spacecraft (above). Although their purpose is mystifying, the account of the event itself is straightforward – putting it in the category of close encounter of the fourth kind known as 'type A'

Right: a Trowbridge man claimed he was awoken by a tall, greenish alien in the early hours of 5 January 1980. The creature said he came from a planet where war is used to control the population level, and that he was trying to prevent the Earth splitting in half by injecting it with cement! This kind of close encounter of the fourth kind, with its obvious conflict with reality, belongs to the category labelled 'type B'

thought, and the station had closed down. Someone or something had stolen a piece of their lives.

The family were naturally perturbed by this mysterious time lapse. Over the next few months they had several dreams about it – fleeting visions of weird faces, occasional strange impulses to refrain from eating meat or drinking alcohol. Eventually two UFO investigators, Andy Collins and Barry King, heard of the event. They brought in the help of a medical hypnotist – Leonard Wilder, a London dentist. The Days underwent regression hypnosis in the hope of retrieving memories of that missing time. And the memories came.

Under hypnosis John and Sue told stories that were in close agreement. However, there

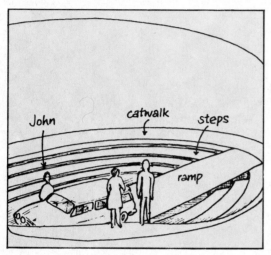

Perhaps the strangest category of close encounter of the fourth kind is that known as 'type C' – where the witnesses are subject to loss of memory following their experience. The Day family of Aveley, Essex, England, underwent this after the events of one October night in 1974. They were driving home when, they claimed, they encountered a UFO (left) that interfered with their car radio – so much, at least, they remembered afterwards. But when they arrived home, they found it was two hours later than they thought – and it subsequently emerged under hypnosis that they believed that they had been taken aboard a UFO by aliens (below) and subjected to medical examinations

were some differences, and they did indeed claim to have been separated for much of the 'missing' time. The children also seemed to recall the experience in subsequent dreams.

A UFO had landed and the family had been taken on board. They were given medical examinations and shown around the craft. They were informed about its propulsion system and the way of life and intentions of the alien visitors. Eventually they were returned to their car by a process akin to astral projection, and they continued their journey. But their lives could never be the same again.

To those who interviewed them, the Day family seemed a group of pleasant and sincere people who had never tried to force their story onto anyone, or to make money from it. Something quite certainly happened to them that night . . . but what?

In type C contacts, something blocks the witnesses' memory. Occasionally recall of the 'missing' events is triggered by normal events. Not infrequently the subject has dreams that hint at what took place during the missing minutes, hours – or even, in a very few instances, days. But the most common means by which the floodgates of memory are opened is regression hypnosis.

Type C abductions are remarkably consistent. One in five stories of alien contact involves amnesia and alleged abduction.

Type C cases are more subjective than ordinary UFO sightings, since they tend to involve fewer witnesses; but they have a higher number of witnesses per case than type B or, surprisingly, type A cases. The aliens involved usually resemble human beings and are usually the normal human size, or larger; there are very few entities of small stature, unlike those featured in type A cases. The most common time for type C incidents to occur is between about 10 p.m. and midnight. And a very large proportion of them involve young couples driving cars along quiet roads (quite often carrying children with them). It is also common for one or more of the witnesses to have a history of strange experiences – witnessing ghosts or poltergeists, for example. And the way of life of the subjects may undergo drastic changes, even before the memory of an apparent abduction is at last retrieved and the cause of the changes made apparent.

The fourth group of close encounters of the fourth kind comprises very few cases. It consists of those experiences in which the encounter does not seem to involve physical contact: communication is by means of telepathy, automatic writing, or something of the kind. We shall not discuss these in this series of chapters. We shall try instead to see whether among all the details of the cases of types A, B and C there is a clue to the reasons why such experiences occur.

Creatures from inner space?

Have beings from other worlds met and talked with people of Earth – or are they creations of the subconscious mind?

HYPNOSIS IS STILL A CONTROVERSIAL subject. Its significance becomes even more obscure when it is used to recover the blocked memories of a witness in a UFO contact case. Experts dispute the origin of the images that come to the mind of such a person in a hypnotic trance. Is the subject's psychic potential boosted? Does he become able to dredge information from the collective unconscious, potentially becoming aware of everything that has ever happened anywhere at all? Or is the abduction memory that comes to the witness simply a respinning by his mind of a story once read and now forgotten – the re-creation of a modern myth? For certainly alien beings and their spacecraft have attained the commanding status of myths of our time, whatever the reality that lies behind them (see page 426). Or does regression hypnosis simply free the

memory so that the barriers to recall can be hurdled and the 'missing' period relived? There is a very difficult problem of assessment whenever a witness in a type C case retrieves a 'memory'. What is its true significance?

A case similar to that of the Day family (see page 74) occurred in June 1978, again in England. A young couple, their children and another adult were involved. The alleged abduction took place during a car journey in Oxfordshire; again there were many similarities with other abduction stories: for example, three-dimensional ('holographic') shows were displayed to the witnesses. But the story as a whole was quite unlike any of the 100 or more other type C cases that have been documented by ufologists. The aliens looked humanoid – indeed, very like those seen by John and Sue Day – and they told of the origin of their race on Earth and their emigration to the planet Janos. Now a horrific natural disaster had precipitated their flight back to Earth. They wish to move in with us . . . a million or so refugees from this cosmic catastrophe.

What is interesting about this case is, partly, how it resembles in outline other incidents, such as the Day case (which had received publicity in the British press). But

Above: life on Jupiter, as imagined by the astronomer Carl Sagan. Herds of floating creatures, little more than living gas-bags, drift above the towering clouds of frozen ammonia crystals in the planet's atmosphere. Some of these beings are visible in the foreground and at the left. It is possible that living creatures have evolved to this level on many planets, but beings capable of building spaceships are much less probable

Overleaf: Gaynor Sunderland, a Welsh girl who has reported numerous encounters with aliens. On one occasion two strange beings allegedly from another planet, visited her and told her that they were products of her own subconscious mind. Other members of Gaynor's family have reported alien contacts

more importantly, the interests, attitudes and manner of questioning of the investigators found their way into the story that was told – as if the hypnotised witnesses were picking up 'cues' from the investigators and fitting them into their accounts as they told them. This is rather like the game in which you are given a series of objects – say, a book, a pen, a candlestick and a toy balloon – and are asked to use your imagination to weave a story in which they all figure.

This curious problem is further illustrated by the experiences of young Gaynor Sunderland, from Oakenholt in North Wales. She and her family had many weird encounters, including contacts with aliens who, again, looked rather like the ones met by others who reported similar experiences.

On one occasion Gaynor was having trouble sleeping because she kept seeing two aliens – one male, one female. (Later she found that they were named Pars and Arna.) I was then investigating the case and I suggested to her mother, Marion Sunderland, that she could tell Gaynor a white lie. Gaynor was told: 'If you put a loaded camera in the bedroom the aliens will not come because they do not like having their pictures taken.' A couple of nights later Gaynor was allegedly abducted to another world and taken on a tour of a city there by Arna and Pars. She was told that she was not really there: the experience was in her subconscious mind, a kind of dream. Yet the aliens maintained: 'We did not come to you because of the camera.'

It is highly paradoxical that an alien entity should first admit to being a product of the unconscious mind and then claim to dislike being photographed. It seems that Gaynor's mind somehow wove the idea concerning the camera into her experience of the trip to another world. But she remained convinced of the reality of her experience and said it was far more vivid than a typical dream.

We sometimes find that the initial stimulus for an abduction experience is an event that can be explained straightforwardly.

Above: the encounter of Betty and Barney Hill with a mysterious craft in September 1961 is a classic contact case. The Hills' recollections of being taken on board the craft emerged later, first in dreams and subsequently in regression hypnosis

This casts doubt on the remainder of the account provided by the witnesses. One of the most famous type C cases involved an American couple, Betty and Barney Hill, who were returning from holiday across the mountains of New England during September 1961. A mysterious 'craft' followed them and then came down nearby; Barney Hill watched it through binoculars before driving away in panic. All the classic features of such incidents were there: a psychic witness (Betty had experienced many types of weird phenomena throughout her life); a blank in their memory of events; strange dreams afterwards; and finally, under hypnosis, memories of abduction and medical examination on board the UFO. Yet it has been argued very convincingly that the light in the sky that marked the beginning of the whole train of events was nothing more than the planet Jupiter.

This does not in itself tell us anything about the reality of the experience; witnesses often link completely unassociated events in their recollections of some incident, simply because those events happened to occur at roughly the same time. But it is just part of the process by which human beings misperceive events, distort their memories of them, and come to mistaken conclusions

about them later. We should bear this complex process of interpretation and misinterpretation in mind as we consider the appearance presented by aliens and their craft in contact reports.

What should we expect extra-terrestrial life forms to look like? This is a very hard question to answer, since our only examples of life come from one planet – the Earth. Yet when we see the amazing range of species hosted by our environment and recognise that mankind is just a link in a long evolutionary chain in which an even greater diversity of forms has existed, we find little reason to suppose that alien beings should look like us. Admittedly the humanoid form is well-adapted to a wide range of environments on the Earth's surface, and it may well be common on other Earth-like planets throughout the Galaxy; but the human form is presumably not a necessary condition for dominance. Since other worlds would have a great range of habitats, and local conditions would vary greatly, life there would undoubtedly be equally diverse. Carl Sagan, the eminent astronomer, has even proposed

Six types of alien being reported by contact case witnesses. These pictures should be viewed as symbolising the various categories, not as accurately portraying any particular entity encountered by a witness. The majority of beings reported are human or humanoid in form – and also remarkably human in their clothing and technology. 'Monsters' are rare. (The 'apparitional' entities come under the heading of type D – 'psychic' – encounters.) Images such as these are firmly stamped into popular consciousness by science fiction films and comics, which may thereby influence perceptions during contact experiences

usually about 3½ feet (1 metre); medium – 5 to 6 feet (1.5 to 1.8 metres); and large – up to about 7 or 8 feet (2.1 to 2.4 metres). In type B ('bedroom visitors') encounters, the entities witnessed are fairly normal, with a slight tendency to larger sizes. In no fewer than 41 per cent of type A cases, on the other hand, the entities seen are small. There are other fairly common features, such as large eyes, fair skins, and angular features. But other factors, such as clothes, show great diversity.

One might not consider this to be a problem. After all, people on Earth wear a wide variety of clothes, and human beings of different ages, races and sexes are extraordinarily diverse. But the difficulty with contact cases is more fundamental: the aliens as described are just too much like us. They usually speak the language of the contactee, whether it be English or Serbo-Croat. Nearly always they speak it faultlessly, and without any noticeable accent. This means, of course, that they are speaking in the same accent as the contactee himself (a vital, but usually overlooked, point).

Their fashions, too, are far too similar to those on Earth. It seems nonsensical to imagine that an alien from a planet light years away should wear a cloak buttoned at the neck and sport a badge on the breast of a jumpsuit-style garment. Yet this is what contactees claim, and it is all too reminiscent of the limited imaginations (or wardrobe budgets) of science fiction film makers.

If a witness asks for the origins of an alien, he is almost invariably told that the entity comes from space. In the earliest contacts the aliens' home planets belonged to our solar system – Mars, Venus, Saturn and so on. Now we know that humanoid life on these worlds is impossible, and present-day contactees are told the aliens come from planets circling distant stars. As yet, of course, science knows little about the very existence of such planets, let alone their suitability for life.

What is it like inside an alien craft? The witnesses' answers to this question also raise

human

humanoid

animal

possible life forms capable of surviving on Jupiter: such as living balloons in the oceans of water that may exist in the warm depths of the planet, below the perpetually frozen clouds that we see.

The last thing we would expect is a menagerie of alien races looking more or less like us – and yet, according to contactees, this is precisely what we do find.

Only 7 per cent of contact cases involve creatures that are not humanoid. Such beings as the giant white maggots that crawled across a road in Yssandon, France, in 1960, during a UFO sighting, are rare.

There are three distinct groupings among the humanoids that form the bulk of the data: small – below 5 feet (1.5 metres) tall, and

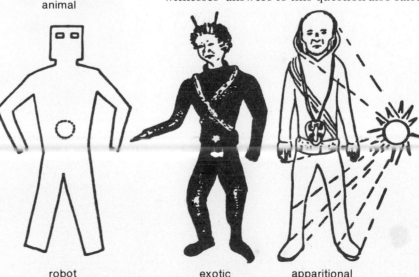

robot

exotic

apparitional

grave questions about the nature of their experience. Imagine a Stone Age man transported through time and taken onto the flight deck of a Concorde airliner. The instruments and controls would be quite incomprehensible to him. How could he possibly describe what he saw in any intelligible way, knowing nothing of the purpose and importance of what he was seeing? This would be the predicament of any Earth-dweller taken inside an alien starship.

Yet these amazingly advanced visitors, who traverse interstellar space at a whim, apparently do so in spaceships that would not look out of place in one of our engineering museums. They use levers and valves, wires, and old-fashioned bulky computers. They have flashing lights, in the manner of *Star Trek* and *Doctor Who*. They are slow in catching up with our primitive technology. They are just getting round to using lasers and holograms (which they did not have before we did), and they do not as yet have the liquid crystal displays that are now standard on our watches and calculators. What is more, their spaceships are always breaking down. . . .

Not infrequently the aliens enlist the help of Earth-dwellers to sort out their problems. Once they asked an eight-year-old boy to fix their propulsion unit. Evidently the origin of all this is not the face-value explanation beloved of the alien spacecraft theorists.

Under alien eyes

Once the contactees are aboard, the aliens usually carry out a medical examination. Taking blood samples is an integral part of this. The Irish ufologist John Hind points out that the doctor is the symbol of authority who plays the greatest role in the lives of many people. There seem to be significant resemblances between these examinations by aliens and the contactees' previous experience of medical treatment. One Canadian abduction appeared to feature a replay of an appendicectomy that the witness had earlier undergone.

The memory blocks in type c cases present an interesting problem. If aliens can suppress memories, why do they do it in such an ineffective way? The memories usually filter through spontaneously and are easily retrievable in full by hypnosis. Why block them at all? Unless the memory block in fact works successfully in most cases – implying that there are thousands of people who are abducted and have no inkling of the fact afterwards.

Whatever the reason for these memory blocks, the lapse of time between the original occurrence and its subsequent recall severely impedes the investigation of the case. And this, of course, may be the most significant function that the memory loss serves.

When aliens give us messages they are almost always of one form: warnings about the future of the Earth, with hints of nuclear war and impending doom. If only we were sometimes given something startling and original – a new scientific theory, a helpful invention, a cure for cancer. But no; we are told that, because of our nuclear tests, 'the balance of the Universe is being disturbed.'

Occasionally there is some light relief. In spring 1978 a Red Army officer was abducted by the shores of the Pyrogovskoye Lake in Russia. Once he had got used to his humanoid hosts, he suggested they ought to toast this cross-cultural contact with a suitable drink. They did not understand. So he sketched out the chemical structure of alcohol, and the aliens retired and immediately made some. 'How is it that such a highly developed civilisation does not use something like this?' the Russian asked. 'Maybe if we had used it we would not be so highly developed,' was the response.

A teetotal message in the form of a joke makes a welcome change from the usual run of communications from other worlds.

In a spaceship from a distant star system, a gigantic robot towers over a prone human form. In this scene from the 1951 film *The day the Earth stood still* the robot, Gort, is bringing its dead master, Klaatu, back to life – but this powerful image epitomises, and may have done much to influence, a whole class of contact case reports: the medical examination of abducted witnesses on board alien craft

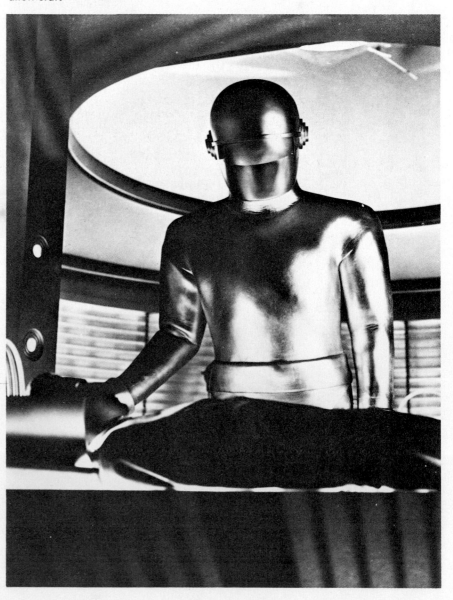

Alien spacecraft, hallucinations or fraud? The theories about UFO contact cases are legion. This chapter assesses each explanation and concludes that the phenomenon lies outside our usual categories of thought

Stranger than fiction

ALIENS BEINGS MUST EXIST – somewhere in the Universe, in some form or other. Of this there is little doubt. The problem confronting us is whether the evidence we possess proves that some of these aliens are visiting the Earth now. If this is so, then proving the fact would be of the utmost significance. It would be perhaps the most momentous occasion in the history of the world.

But we do not possess photographs, movie films or tape recordings of aliens, or artefacts manufactured on another world . . . anything that goes beyond mere testimony. In view of this paucity of hard evidence we can hardly say, with any definiteness, whether aliens are or are not visiting us. We can only make a reasoned assessment of the facts.

The dilemmas posed by close encounters of the fourth kind are starkly illustrated by a case that occurred in the north of England on 28 November 1980. Police Constable Alan Godfrey had been called out to pursue some cows that were allegedly roaming a housing estate. By 5.15 a.m., still not having found them, he was ready to give up the search. While making one last trip in his patrol car before coming off duty, he saw a glow on the road ahead. He instantly thought of a works bus that regularly travelled the route and idly wondered why it was a little early. Then, as he approached the glow, it became obvious that he had been wrong.

The object that confronted PC Godfrey was like a spinning top with windows. It was hovering just above the road surface, spanning the gap between two lamp posts, and it was rotating. He could see his headlights reflected in the metallic surface of the object. He could see leaves on the roadside bushes moving in the vortex created by its rotation. The road surface, soaking wet in other places, was dry in blotchy patches directly beneath the object. There was no doubt in his mind that the object was real.

Maintaining the traditional calm of the British 'bobby', the officer propped his clipboard on the windscreen and carefully sketched the object. But then something inexplicable happened. He suddenly found himself further down the road, driving the car away from the scene. Nonplussed, he turned the car round and drove past the spot, now deserted, where the object had been. He carried on the short distance into town and collected a colleague. Only at this point did he notice the time. Somewhere, since the moment he first saw the UFO, 10 minutes had disappeared.

Constable Godfrey had a dim memory, however – of a strange voice saying: 'This is not for your eyes. You will forget it.' Additional fragmentary recollections gradually

filtered back to him until, nine months after the incident, and with the help of ufologists, he underwent regression hypnosis. This was conducted by an eminently qualified and rather sceptical psychiatrist, and what appeared to be a coherent memory of the incident emerged.

The story was of the usual type: the officer had been taken on board the UFO and given a medical examination by two distinct types of humanoid creature – one tall, the other small and somewhat ugly. Remarkably, this is almost exactly what the Day family claimed happened to them during their abduction at Aveley in Essex (see page 74). In fact, contact cases reported from Britain share such similarities in many features. Cases reported from other countries, on the other hand, show different similarities among themselves.

What happened to the police constable? Is he lying to us? If not, did he have an hallucination or did he undergo the events he described? Or was it something between hallucination and straightforward experience – a distortion or misinterpretation of some extraordinary events?

There happens to be unusual and powerful support for the 'face-value' interpretation of the story. Four police officers on patrol 8 miles (13 kilometres) away had to duck as a UFO streaked low over their heads, moving directly towards the town near which the encounter took place. And a caretaker lighting a school's boilers saw in the direction of the town an object that fitted PC Godfrey's description, climbing into the sky. These stories were reported independently while the police officer was still reporting what he had just observed.

When faced with an issue like this, most people take sharply contrasting attitudes. Some would want to believe that aliens were involved. Others would deny that this was possible, and would cling to the hallucination theory. Unfortunately these two hypotheses have points both in their favour and against them. So let us survey some of the difficulties that the various answers face.

Why do aliens look like us? Why do they behave like us? Why do they mirror our social and scientific developments? Why do they never tell us anything valuable to which we do not already have access? These problems are curiously like those involved in alleged memories of past lives, spirit messages and other demonstrations of survival of death. It is surely not without significance that the common factor in these cases is the frequent use of regression hypnosis and the role of the human mind. Taken together, these facts suggest a mental origin for these strange experiences.

Between waking and sleep

To this type of evidence we should add research into lucid dreams. These are dreams in which the dreamer is fully aware that he is dreaming. Often the course of the dream can be controlled by conscious effort. Such dreams are rare and seem to overlap with such phenomena as hypnagogic imagery (the images, often compellingly 'real', that come when we are between waking and sleep).

Although they seem so real at the time, lucid dreams and hypnagogic images give away their 'unreal' nature in various subtle hints. For example, the subject does not react with normal responses. He may feel no fear, despite the weirdness of the experience. He will not wake up a sleeping bed partner to witness the events. In one case a person had such an experience, in which he thought an atomic bomb had just exploded in his garden. His response was to yawn and fall asleep. The behaviour of contact case witnesses is often like this.

Interestingly, such symptoms also occur in hallucinations that follow long periods of sensory deprivation. When a person is kept in darkness and silence, and even his sense of touch is deprived of its normal stimulation because his hands are enveloped in special gloves, his mind starts to manufacture its own 'perceptions' – hallucinations of sound, sight and touch. When we consider the usual setting of a type C contact – night-time, a tired driver, a lonely country road, and the sudden appearance of a slightly unusual sight, such as a bright light in the sky – it does not stretch credulity very far to suggest that these could be hallucinations brought about by the lack of sensory stimulation.

In the USA Dr Alvin Lawson, a professor of

Previous page, top: in the north of England a craft resembling a spinning top hovers above a road. The witness – a police constable. Later he recalled an experience of being taken aboard the craft and examined by terrifying creatures

Previous page, bottom: Alan Godfrey, the police constable who believes he was taken aboard an alien craft in November 1980, standing at the scene of the incident. The ufonauts who abducted him included, he said, eight small 'robots'

Words of wisdom

Surveying 16 years of editing *Flying Saucer Review*, Charles Bowen, a contributor to *The Unexplained*, commented on the rich absurdities of the UFO occupants' messages. In 1968 in Argentina two 'men' with transparent legs gave a farmer's son a written message that may be rendered as: 'You shall know the world. F. Saucer.' In 1965 in Venezuela two beings 7 to 8 feet (2.1 to 2.4 metres) tall, with long yellow hair and protruding eyes, were asked whether there were 'any human beings like you living among us?' The answer was: 'Yes. 2,417,805.' (Surely one of them will be spotted soon!) During the 1954 'flap' a French witness encountered a small being standing before a glowing disc-shaped craft. The alien repeated several times in a 'mechanical' voice: '*La veritée est refusée aux constipés,*' and: '*Ce que vous appelez cancer vient des dents.*' Translated, these messages from another civilisation read: 'Truth is denied to the constipated' (or: 'to the ill at ease'), and: 'That which is known as cancer comes from the teeth' (or: 'through what you eat').

We can't say we weren't warned.

The trouble with hypnosis

In 1977 Professor Alvin Lawson began to investigate the validity of UFO abduction reports obtained under hypnosis. He hypnotised a total of 16 volunteers who knew very little about UFOs. Once in trance, they were asked to imagine a series of events – seeing a UFO, being taken on board, given an examination and so on. Lawson hoped to find differences between their imaginary accounts and those given by alleged UFO contactees. Such differences would enhance the credibility of the 'real' reports.

To his surprise, it was the similarities that were most striking. For example, among his test subjects' narratives were descriptions of 'tubes of light', which extended from UFOs or retracted into them, perhaps 'levitating' the subject aboard. Sometimes the subject described the UFO as 'getting bigger and smaller'. And patterns of pulsating colours, rotating spirals and geometric patterns were often reported. All these features are common in 'real' UFO reports, but they are rare in science fiction stories and films, a likely source of UFO imagery.

The experiments showed that authentic-sounding reports could be produced in abundance by subjects who have never claimed to have been abducted by a UFO. Dr Lawson concluded that contact case witnesses were not lying – but he could offer no hypothesis as to the nature of the stimulus causing their experience.

English at the University of California, has conducted experiments that are relevant to the hallucination theory. He advertised for people of a 'creative' turn of mind to take part in an unspecified experiment. He screened out all those who seemed to have a knowledge of, or interest in, UFOs. The rest were asked to imagine, under hypnosis, that they were being abducted by aliens. They were led on with certain key questions, and the results, he claimed, were so closely akin to the stories told of allegedly real abductions that it was likely that these also were, wholly or in part, subconscious fantasies.

These different types of evidence constitute impressive support for the contention that alien contacts are hallucinatory. But unfortunately there is a fair amount of negative evidence too. Some contact experiences are shared; while collective hallucinations can occur, they are not well-understood, and some encounters stretch this hypothesis to breaking point. One Italian type A case involved seven witnesses; one British type A involved four. In some cases, such as those in Puerto Rico and that involving the English police officer, there is at least some degree of *independent* corroboration.

Alvin Lawson's work, as he himself recognised, showed major differences between allegedly real abductions and imagined ones, as well as similarities. When, in a UFO contact case, memories emerge by way of hypnosis, they are almost invariably associated with very strong emotions, more consistent with the memory of a real event than a fantasy. The 'abductions' imagined in the laboratory did not display this effect, and in general those who took part in the experiment knew afterwards that they had been fantasising. Contact witnesses are never in any doubt that their regression memory is of a real event. It can still be argued, of course, that the remembered event, though real, is purely 'mental' – an hallucination or dream.

We must also consider the frequent reports of physical effects on a witness's body,

Right: more outlandish than most descriptions of aliens provided by UFO contactees: Alpha Centauri, a well-dressed science fiction monster from the television series *Dr Who*. 'Real' ufonauts are far more similar to human beings – or to gnomes, giants, dwarves and other 'traditional' mythical creatures

Left: two high officials of the Draconian race – another instance of the television designer's imagination outstripping the diversity of reported aliens. Animal forms, or hybrid animal-human forms like these, might be expected among ufonauts – whether they were genuinely extra-terrestrial or the products of the human imagination. In fact, both 'real' accounts and 'imaginary' ones produced under laboratory conditions are seldom of this type

such as burns on the skin. Marks on the ground sometimes accompany these cases as well. But, on the other hand, there is almost no photographic support for the contact witnesses' stories – and physical effects can be produced psychosomatically.

Looking at more subtle features of the accounts, considerable consistency and a kind of lucid cohesiveness appear in all but the type B 'bedroom visitor' cases. This tends to make the UFO investigator doubt that he is dealing with experiences more akin to dreams than reality.

It is very difficult to sort out these contradictory elements. Perhaps the fairest judgement we can make at present is to say that type B experiences *seem* more like vivid hallucinations than reality. Type C ('memory block') cases have elements suggesting hallucinations but, unlike type B experiences, offer some data that cast doubt on this assumption. If type C cases are indeed hallucinations, they seem to be of a unique type – almost a hybrid between dream and reality. As for the most common contact cases, type A, they are the least like hallucinations. While they are full of problems, we cannot explain them as hallucinations with any degree of confidence.

What of the other extreme? Are these contacts extra-terrestrial in nature? This, the 'face-value' hypothesis, implies that hundreds of different races (most of them not very imaginative variants on ourselves), from many different worlds, are taking a great deal of interest in the Earth. They perform medical examinations interminably, and gather up endless cargoes of soil and rock samples. For no apparent reason the Earth is the Galaxy's Grand Central Station.

The sceptics invariably ask why the aliens

Of the six drawings below, three were made by witnesses in UFO contact cases, and were offered as *bona fide* representations of alien beings. The others were made by participants in Alvin Lawson's 'simulated abduction' experiments. These subjects, though they produced their accounts under hypnosis, were never in doubt about the imaginary nature of their experiences. Is there a different 'feel' about the two types of drawing? Can you pick out the three 'real' contact witness drawings? The answer is printed at the lower right

don't contact someone important. Why not land on the White House lawn and thus dispel all doubts?

Gaynor Sunderland (see page 80) asked Arna, one of the aliens she claimed to have met, this very question. She was told that people in authority had so much credibility to lose that there was no point in contacting them, although this had been tried on a few occasions. Fear of the consequences kept such people silent. Instead the aliens pursue a policy of contacting children or simple folk, knowing that some of these will brave the ridicule and speak out.

This argument makes an intriguing amount of sense. Widespread belief in the existence of alien life is the only tangible result of decades of UFO stories. A slow, covert process of conditioning world opinion to the idea of extra-terrestrial visitors fits well with the 'provocative but not probative' evidence that we possess. Solid proof would be detrimental to such a policy: it would be impounded, or hidden, or denied outright. Suggestive indications, on the other hand, avoid the unwelcome attention of authority while providing a stimulus to continued interest and promoting the long, slow build-up of belief. Even the confusing and ridiculous behaviour of the aliens would fit this theory. In the end the only people who will not be convinced that aliens come from space will be the UFO investigators themselves!

A great deal of fascinating work remains before we can hope to know the truth. There is no hard evidence that a superior intelligence has made contact with the Earth – but we do have suggestive hints that this *might* be true. And, since most of us would wish UFOs to come from space, our judgement is clouded by an enormous emotional bias.

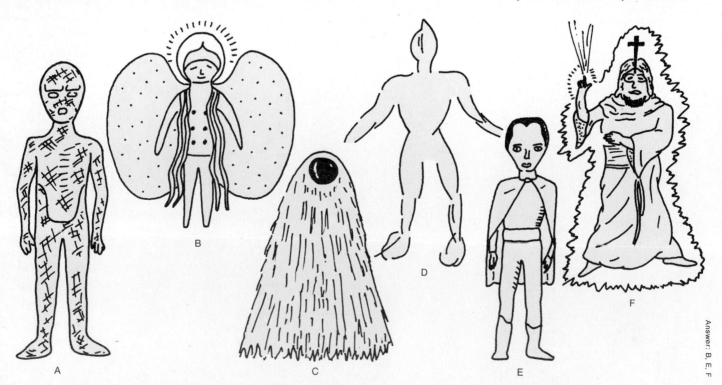

A   B   C   D   E   F

Answer: B, E, F

Cergy-Pontoise

Three young Frenchmen hit the news headlines in early December 1979 with a tale about a UFO abduction at Cergy-Pontoise. But was their amazing story a fabrication? HILARY EVANS sorts out the facts from the fiction

'FRENCHMAN BACK TO EARTH with a bump' was the headline in the London *Times* – and across the world the media reported the news with the same uncertainty whether to take it seriously or not. But this much was certain: Franck Fontaine, who had allegedly been kidnapped by a UFO a week before, had been restored to friends, family, and a wondering world in the early hours of Monday, 3 December 1979.

Where had he spent those seven days? The world, hoping for a story that would make the Moon landing seem tame, was disappointed. Fontaine's recollections were few and confused. It seemed to him he had simply dropped off to sleep for half an hour: he was astonished and dismayed to find he had been away for a week. He attributed the strange images in his mind to dreams: he was bewildered to learn that he might have been abducted by extra-terrestrial aliens and carried to their distant world.

Police search a field in Cergy-Pontoise, France, for clues to the disappearance of Franck Fontaine, reported as having been abducted by a UFO. Fontaine's two friends, Jean-Pierre Prévost and Salomon N'Diaye, said they had witnessed the kidnapping early one morning in late November 1979. In the background is the block of flats in which Prévost and N'Diaye lived and near which the event occurred

Fontaine was no less dismayed to find himself the focus of the world's attention. During his seven-day absence, it had been his friends Salomon N'Diaye and Jean-Pierre Prévost, witnesses of his abduction, who had been the objects of attention. Ever since their first startling telephone call to the police – 'A friend of mine's just been carried off by a UFO!' – they had been subjected to interrogation by the police, by the press, and by UFO investigative groups ranging from the scientific to the bizarre. If Fontaine's return brought renewed publicity and fresh problems, at least it cleared them of the suspicion that they were responsible for their friend's disappearance – perhaps even his death.

The life-style of the three young men was not of a sort to dispel suspicion. All three – Prévost, aged 26, N'Diaye, 25, Fontaine, 18 – scraped an uncertain living by selling jeans in street markets. They drove an old car that was unlicensed and uninsured, none of them having a driving licence. Prévost was a self-declared anarchist. He and N'Diaye lived next door to each other in a modern block at Cergy-Pontoise on the outskirts of Paris. Fontaine lived 2 miles (3 kilometres) away.

According to their account, Fontaine had

Mystery of the lost week

spent Sunday evening in Prévost's flat because they wanted to be up by 3.30 a.m. to travel the 35 miles (60 kilometres) to the street market at Gisors. The market didn't start until 8 a.m. but they wanted a good place. Besides, their Taunus estate car had been acting up lately, so they thought it prudent to allow extra time. At 3.30, after only about four hours' sleep, they were up and ready to load the car with clothes.

First, though, they gave the car a push-start to make sure the engine would function. Having got it going, they decided that Fontaine should stay in the car to make sure it didn't stop again while the other two got on with the loading. Fontaine had leisure to look about him, and so it was that he noticed a brilliant light in the sky some distance away. When his companions arrived with their next

load, he pointed the object out. It was cylindrical in shape, but otherwise unidentifiable. When it moved behind the block of flats, N'Diaye rushed upstairs to fetch a camera, thinking he might take a photograph of the object to sell to the newspapers. Prévost went in to get another load of clothing while Fontaine, hoping for another view of the mysterious object, drove up onto the main road that ran close by the flats.

Hearing the sound of the moving vehicle, his companions looked out of the windows of their respective flats. Both saw that Fontaine had stopped the car on the main road and noted that the engine was no longer running. Prévost, angry because they would probably have to push-start the car a second time, rushed downstairs again. He called to N'Diaye to forget about his camera because the UFO had vanished. N'Diaye came after him saying that in any case he had no film in his camera, and adding that from his window it had looked as though the car was surrounded by a great ball of light.

Outdoors again, the two young men stopped in amazement: the rear of their car was

Top: Franck Fontaine leaving the police station after being questioned upon his safe return. He said that his 'missing week' was a blank in his mind

Salomon N'Diaye (above) and Jean-Pierre Prévost (right) reported the UFO incident to the police at once – a fact that convinced many they were telling the truth

enveloped in a sharply defined sphere of glowing mist, near which a number of smaller balls of light were moving about. While they stood watching, they saw the larger globe absorb all but one of the smaller ones. Then a beam of light emerged, which grew in size until it was like the cylindrical shape they had seen earlier. The large sphere seemed to enter this cylinder, which shot up into the sky and disappeared from sight.

The two hurried to the car, but found no sign of Fontaine. He was not in the car, in the road, or in the cabbage field beside the road. Prévost insisted on calling the police immediately and N'Diaye went off to do so. Prévost, remaining near the car, was the only witness to the last phase of the incident: a ball of light, like those previously moving about

the car, seemed to push the car door shut. Then it too vanished.

Such was the account that the two young men gave to the police on their arrival a few minutes later. Because UFO sightings are a military matter in France, the police instructed Prévost and N'Diaye to inform the gendarmerie, which comes under the Ministry of National Defence. The two spent most of the day with the gendarmes, telling and retelling the story. The interrogators stopped for lunch, during which time the witnesses telephoned the press with their story. Later, Commandant Courcoux of the Cergy gendarmerie told the press that there were no grounds for disbelieving the young men's story, that he had no doubt 'something' had occurred, and that he could give no indication of what that 'something' might be. In a later interview he admitted, 'We are swimming in fantasy.'

For a week, that was all the world knew. During that week, the young men were questioned over and over again. Some people accepted the UFO story as it stood. Others suspected it to be a smokescreen, perhaps a cunning plan to help Fontaine avoid doing his military service, perhaps something more sinister. But one fact stood out clearly: Prévost and N'Diaye had informed the police promptly and voluntarily. Given their backgrounds, wasn't this convincing proof of their sincerity?

When Fontaine gave his version of the story, there seemed no reason to question his sincerity either. He told how he had woken to find himself lying in the cabbage field. Getting to his feet, he realised he was just across the main road from the flats, close to where he had stopped the car to watch the UFO. But the car was no longer there. His first thought,

Jimmy Guieu, well-known science fiction writer and founder of a UFO group. The trio put themselves into his hands exclusively; other UFO investigators found them to be very unco-operative

as he hurried towards the still-darkened building, was that somebody had stolen their car and its valuable load of clothing. Neither Prévost nor N'Diaye was to be seen, so he rushed upstairs and rang the bell of Prévost's flat. When there was no reply, he went to N'Diaye's. A sleepy N'Diaye appeared, gawped at him in amazement, then flung his arms round him in delighted welcome. Fontaine, already surprised to find his friend in his night clothes, was even more amazed to learn that an entire week had gone by since the morning of the Gisors market.

He had little to tell the press or the police. The world's media reported his return but reserved judgement till they heard what the authorities had to say. But the police declared it was no longer their business: no crime had been committed. Apart from the inherent improbability of Fontaine's story, they had no reason to doubt his word or that of his friends.

Besieged by ufologists

So now it was up to the UFO organisations to see what further light could be thrown on the case. From the start, the witnesses had been besieged by the various French groups; there are dozens of these, most of them fiercely independent and reluctant to co-operate with the others. One of the most reputable of all is Control, to whom we owe most of what we now know of the inside story of the Cergy-Pontoise case.

But another group declared its interest before Control, while Fontaine was still missing: the *Institut Mondial des Sciences Avancés* (World Institute of Advanced Sciences). Its co-founder and spokesman was the well-known science fiction writer and author of two books about UFOs, Jimmy

Right: the cylinder-shaped UFO seen by the three friends appeared to have a diameter larger than that of the full Moon that night. It had a rounded front end and a tail that trailed off into a hazy cloud. It was when Fontaine went closer to the UFO – alone – that he disappeared

Guieu. Before he had carried out an investigation, Guieu affirmed his belief in the story: 'No question of it, Franck Fontaine has been abducted on board a UFO,' he stated in an interview. 'Admittedly I haven't questioned the young man's two companions, but I hold their account to be true a priori.'

Delighted to have their story accepted without reservation by so eminent an authority, Fontaine's two friends agreed to co-operate with Guieu. When Fontaine returned, he too was taken under IMSA's wing. Guieu offered them a secret refuge in the south of France where they could work on a book together, Guieu writing it and all sharing the proceeds.

Guieu's book, *Cergy-Pontoise UFO contacts*, was rushed into print with astonishing speed, appearing a bare four months after Fontaine's return. Thanks to the combination of Guieu's name and the intense interest in the case, it was an instant bestseller. But readers hoping for a conclusive verdict were disappointed. The book was padded out by Guieu's journalistic style and digressive accounts of other cases, and there was an almost total absence of first-hand testimony from the principal witness – the abducted Fontaine – whose story the world wanted to hear. Such revelations as the book contained were of quite another nature.

Guieu had hoped that Fontaine would be able to recall more of his adventure if he were

Jimmy Guieu's book *Cergy-Pontoise UFO contacts* (top) and Jean-Pierre Prévost's book *The truth about the Cergy-Pontoise affair* (above). Both were published speedily after the alleged kidnapping of Franck Fontaine. Both were long on fantasy and short on facts, disappointing all who hoped for some clarification of what had really happened

hypnotised, but the young man obstinately refused to submit to hypnosis. Then Prévost suggested that he should be hypnotised instead. What resulted was truly amazing. It now emerged that Prévost, not Fontaine, had been the true object of alien interest. Now, speaking through him, the aliens explained all. Fontaine had simply been the means to establish communication: Prévost was the channel through whom they could communicate to help save Earth from impending disaster. The aliens identified themselves as 'the intelligences from beyond' but gave no clearer clue to the whereabouts of 'beyond' than that it is 'a planet not like yours'. Their spokesman was Haurrio, a friendly if somewhat garrulous character.

In Guieu's book, Prévost becomes the hero of the story and the only evidence we have for the events is his word. His two companions seem to have become irrelevant.

This book having raised more questions than it answered, much was hoped for when Prévost announced that he was writing his own account of the event. But *The truth about the Cergy-Pontoise affair*, published later that same year, was even less satisfactory. It was a rambling, incoherent farrago in which great doses of alien 'philosophy' – transmitted by Prévost – show that pious platitudes about the need for more love and less science are not confined to planet Earth.

There is virtually no mention of Franck Fontaine's abduction: indeed, he and Salomon N'Diaye are scarcely referred to. But Prévost's visit to a secret alien base is described in some detail, and this gives us a good yardstick for evaluating the rest of the material. It seems that one morning soon

there. So Prévost, though surprised at the
stranger's offer, cheerfully accepted it. The
salesman dropped him off at the village and
he set off up the hill towards a particular site
that had always fascinated him — a railway
tunnel containing an abandoned train carriage from the Second World War.

Arriving at the tunnel in late evening,
Prévost found that other people were there
before him: a group of young men gathered
round a fire in the open. One of them called
out his name; he was from the Sahara and had
recently written to Prévost. It turned out that
he and the others had come there from many
parts of the world, thanks to the 'intelligences from beyond'. Each spoke his own
language — but was understood by the rest.

When Haurrio, the alien representative,
arrived, he informed them that they had been
chosen to spread the philosophy of the 'intelligences' on Earth. A beautiful female alien
then took them on a tour of the tunnel, now
being used as a UFO base. They saw several
spacecraft, similar to ones that Prévost had
seen as a child. After their tour, the young
men returned to their camp fire and went to
sleep on the ground – which, on a December
night in the mountains, must have been less
than comfortable. Next morning Prévost
found his friendly salesman waiting to chauf-
feur him back to Cergy.

Whether Jimmy Guieu and Jean-Pierre
Prévost seriously expected their accounts to
be believed, we may never know. But the
more they provided in the way of checkable
statements, the harder it became to accept
the original account of the alleged abduction.
Doubts grew even more when an investigative team from Control persisted in taking up
the case without the co-operation of the
witnesses — checking all the conflicting statements and fragmented testimony as best they
could.

after Fontaine's return, there was a ring at
Prévost's door. The caller was a travelling
salesman, a total stranger who said he had to
make a trip to Bourg-de-Sirod and invited
Prévost to come along. Now, Bourg-de-
Sirod is a small village near the Swiss border
some 225 miles (360 kilometres) from Cergy.
On the face of it, there is no conceivable
reason why a salesman should go there, nor
why he should think that Prévost might wish
to go there given that they were strangers in
the first place.

However, there was a reason for interest
by Prévost. Bourg-de-Sirod was a specially
significant place for him because as a child he
had gone to a summer camp nearby and had
later worked there. More recently still, he
and Fontaine had spent a camping holiday

Long after the much-publicised disappearance of Franck Fontaine from Cergy-Pontoise, confusion still reigns over whether he was abducted by a UFO. Was it all a put-up job by him and his two friends? Or did it really happen?

THE ABDUCTION OF Franck Fontaine by a UFO, though unsubstantiated by scientific evidence, seemed a plausible story on first hearing. Had he and his friends Jean-Pierre Prévost and Salomon N'Diaye been content to tell that story and nothing else, they might have convinced an interested world of its truth. But the two books on the case – one by the well-known science fiction writer Jimmy Guieu and one by Prévost himself – raised questions that cast suspicion on the entire affair. Moreover, there were many interviews and conferences in which widely divergent material was put forward. And Prévost, who had pre-empted Fontaine as the hero of the Cergy-Pontoise UFO affair, even published a short-lived journal in which he kept the public informed of his continuing dialogue with the 'intelligences from beyond' who

he claimed had contacted him.

All this increased the doubts of the sceptics. Michel Piccin and his colleagues of the Control organisation had detected inconsistencies and contradictions in the witnesses' statements from the start. And the more they probed, the more discrepancies they found.

It began with trivial, marginal matters, like Prévost's insistence that before the encounter he had no interest in or knowledge of UFOs. The Control investigators found that his brother was a French representative of the American UFO organisation APRO. Even if Prévost did not share his brother's interest in UFOs, he could hardly have been unaware of them. Besides, in his own book, Prévost had said that he saw several spacecraft similar to ones he had 'seen as a child' when the 'intelligences' took him to their UFO base. He also denied seeing a magazine in which a UFO abduction story, very like Fontaine's, was being serialised. Yet Control established that this very magazine was in Prévost's flat at the time of the Cergy-Pontoise abduction.

The events of the night before the abduction became more confused the more they were investigated. Control discovered that there were five people – not three – in

fact, fraud or fantasy?

Prévost's flat that night. Why had the published accounts almost completely failed to mention the presence of Corinne, Prévost's girlfriend, and Fabrice Joly? One reason suggested itself: knowledge of the presence of the fourth young man, Joly, might throw doubt on one of the facts most favourable to Prévost and N'Diaye. They had claimed that they had gone straight to the police when Fontaine vanished from their car, even though they knew they might get into trouble because they were driving without a licence. But Joly was there because he had a valid licence and had agreed to drive the three friends to the market at Gisors.

Discrepancies abound

Why were Corinne and Joly never questioned about what happened? Did they see and hear nothing? They could certainly have straightened out some of the contradictions, for Fontaine, Prévost and N'Diaye could not even agree on who had been at the flat on the night before the abduction – surely one of the most memorable of their lives. First the three had said they spent the night together. Then Prévost recollected that he had watched a television film with friends elsewhere.

Other discrepancies force us to ask how far we can trust their account. They said that they were dubious about their car's ability to start and pushed it to get the motor running, then left Fontaine in the car to make sure it didn't stop. Why didn't Joly, the only licensed driver, do this so that Fontaine could lend a hand with loading the jeans for the market? Did they really sit outside the block of flats at 4 a.m. with the motor running without any complaint from the neighbours? None of the other residents seem even to have heard the sound. What about N'Diaye's completely opposing statement that they

Above: Franck Fontaine, whose disappearance for a week – allegedly as an abductee of aliens – stirred worldwide interest. He was never very forthcoming about what had happened to him

Left: the cabbage field in which Fontaine awoke on his return to Cergy-Pontoise

loaded the car first and only then started the motor? Whom should we believe?

The account of the one neighbour who did witness anything only makes matters more confused. Returning home at the time the young men were supposedly loading the car, he said he saw two people get into the Taunus estate car and drive away. Yet the three involved said that Fontaine was alone when he drove up onto the road to get a better view of the UFO they had spotted.

Even though UFOs are notoriously difficult to describe, the three accounts of the one at Cergy-Pontoise are particularly far apart. One saw 'a huge beam', another 'a ball', the third 'a flash'. One said it was moving fairly slowly, taking two minutes to cross the sky; the others said it was moving fast, gone in a matter of seconds. There was further disagreement about the direction in which it was moving.

The circumstances of Fontaine's return a week after his supposed abduction are no less confused as several stories emerged. One of the journalists covering the case was Iris Billon-Duplan, who worked for a local newspaper and lived close by. Apart from the special interest of a case that had occurred almost on her doorstep, the fact that she lived nearby meant she could follow it personally. As a result, she became closely involved with the witnesses. Indeed, she spent the night before Fontaine's return with Prévost, preparing a definitive account of the case.

According to the journalist's published account, N'Diaye went off to bed shortly after midnight, leaving her with Prévost. He told her that he had no food or money because his involvement in the UFO affair was keeping him from working. So she suggested that they go to her flat where she could give him a meal while they continued to work on

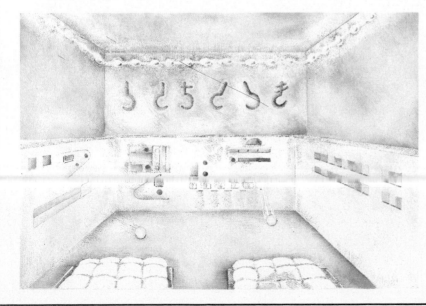

Space briefing

Franck Fontaine remembered things that had happened to him during his week 'out of this world' only slowly and bit by bit, but refused to undergo hypnosis to speed the process. However, strange – and sometimes very disturbing – dreams helped him to recall his experiences, he said.

In one instance that he recalled, he was in a large white room with machines that went all round the walls. They were all the same height and had opaque white glass fronts that lit up and went out almost simultaneously. He was lying on a sort of couch and two small luminous spheres – the extra-terrestrials – were talking to him about problems on Earth and how to solve them.

His abductors, who were always kind, told him that he would be the sole judge of what to reveal of his adventure. He seems to have decided to say as little as possible.

the article. This explains why Fontaine did not find Prévost in when he returned and went to Prévost's flat. We know that Fontaine then went to N'Diaye's flat and succeeded in rousing him. But according to the journalist's account, N'Diaye then left Fontaine and hurried round to her flat to tell her and Prévost the news.

Should we believe Iris Billon-Duplan or Salomon N'Diaye? For his statement, made to the police, flatly contradicts hers.

His story was that he happened to wake up at about 4.30 a.m., looked out of his window and saw a ball of light on the main road. When he saw a silhouetted figure emerge from it, he recognised his friend Franck Fontaine. He then hurried to a telephone to report the return to Radio Luxembourg, believing he would get a reward for information about Fontaine's whereabouts. (In this he was mistaken; it was Europe Numéro 1 that had offered a reward.)

Radio Luxembourg later confirmed that such a call had been made, but not at 4.30 a.m. because there was nobody on duty at that hour. The implication is that N'Diaye telephoned later than 4.30 a.m. and that he waited to inform the police until he had attempted to claim the reward money – not saying much for his concern about his friend. In the event, it was Radio Luxembourg staff who told the police that Franck Fontaine had returned. According to them, they had received an *anonymous* call from a man who, just as he was going to work, saw Fontaine coming back. Surely N'Diaye would not have made an anonymous call if he wanted to collect the reward.

These contradictions are just a sample from Control's 50-page report. There is confusion, if not outright deception, at every stage of the affair. Some of the discrepancies can be attributed to faulty memory, but such an explanation can hardly be stretched to account for Prévost's extraordinary visit to the tunnel. As a case history, Cergy-Pontoise is so ambiguous that few will be ready to give it serious credence. Yet it caused such a sensation that it is still worth asking what really happened. If the abduction was not genuine, was it a put-up job from the outset? Or did the witnesses gradually distort what was fundamentally a true UFO experience? If so, at what point did deceit and contrivance begin? There are several ways to answer these questions.

An elaborate tale

We may believe that Franck Fontaine was abducted as claimed, that all the witnesses were doing their best to tell the truth and that contradictions crept in because of defective memory. However, the extent of the discrepancies makes it easier to believe that the trio elaborated the story for their own purposes, adding sensational details that they may or may not have believed actually happened.

Alternatively, we may surmise that Franck Fontaine was not in fact abducted, but that he sincerely believed he was. He may have been in, or put into, some altered state of consciousness in which he experienced the illusion of the abduction. That this can happen is an established psychological phenomenon, so we cannot rule it out altogether. But it does raise questions about Fontaine's two friends. If he was deluded,

Top: Jean-Pierre Prévost with Patrick Pottier of the Control group. Control carried out as thorough an investigation as they could without the active co-operation of Prévost and the other two involved

Above: Saloman N'Diaye in front of the Taunus estate car which, he said, he and Prévost saw enveloped by a UFO just before their friend Fontaine disappeared

where do they stand? Were they also in an altered state of consciousness, experiencing or being made to believe in the same illusion? And does this explain the contradictions? If so, who fed them the illusion and made them believe in its reality?

While neither of these explanations can be ruled out entirely, we may consider it most plausible that the whole affair was a fabrication from the start – that there never was any abduction and that the three young men put the story together for fun, for gain or for some undiscovered ideological motive. We know that the trio immediately co-operated with Jimmy Guieu in a commercial enterprise. We learn from Control that Prévost, clearly the dominant one of the three, was noted for practical joking at school. Indeed he told the Control investigators, 'You bet I'm a clown!'

More questions than answers

The reports are consistent with the hypothesis that Prévost persuaded his two companions to stage a hoax, but that Corinne and Fabrice Joly refused to go along. Perhaps none of them expected their story to attract so much attention and they were forced to improvise beyond their prepared narrative. This could explain such muddles as the contradictory accounts of Fontaine's return.

Another question then arises: was Guieu a party to the deception? Did he suspect the story from the start but, as a professional writer, recognise its money-making potential? Did he start by believing them, as he claimed to do, then discover the hoax but decide to go along with it – perhaps because he was already committed? Or did he believe that the affair was genuine? The last supposition seems unlikely in the light of Guieu's long involvement with ufology, unless he was unusually gullible. On the other hand, it is hard to believe that he would risk his reputation by endorsing a case that he knew to be a fake. We are probably left with the surmise that he discovered a hoax but decided not to reveal it for reasons of his own.

If the Cergy-Pontoise contact was indeed all a hoax, it would explain why the trio committed themselves to the uncritical Guieu and his *Institut Mondial des Sciences Avancés* (World Institue of Advanced Sciences). IMSA has little following or reputation, but Guieu offered the backing of a big name, sympathetic support and the chance to make a substantial profit from a book bearing his name. And other UFO organisations might have uncovered the deceit in a short time, if deceit it was.

In the absence of any definite proof, all this is merely speculative. Will the truth ever be established? There are hopes that it may be. During their researches, Control came across a tantalising clue that they were unable to follow up. It seems that during Fontaine's disappearance, a school in Cergy-Pontoise was working on a project about it with the local newspaper – the one that was later to carry Iris Billon-Duplan's version of Fontaine's return. Some of the children learned that one of the school workers was an aunt of Fontaine and interviewed her as part of their project in the presence of one of the teachers and one of Iris Billon-Duplan's colleagues from the paper. During the interview, Fontaine's aunt said angrily that she knew perfectly well where her nephew was. He was, she said, staying with a friend.

Was she stating a fact or simply saying what she thought to be true? Who was the friend and where did he or she live? The answers to these questions could settle the Cergy-Pontoise mystery. But until we learn if someone knew where Fontaine was all the time, the case must remain open.

Right: a UFO base in a disused railway tunnel, as described by Jean-Pierre Prévost in his book on the Cergy-Pontoise affair. The tunnel also contained an abandoned Nazi train carriage left over from the Second World War. Prévost, always the dominant member of the trio of witnesses, quickly became the 'star of the show' and the other two receded into the background – for, said Prévost, the aliens had simply used Fontaine to establish contact with himself

Index

PRINTED IN BELGIUM BY

proost
INTERNATIONAL BOOK PRODUCTION